Letters to Myself
Volume 3
Addiction

By:
Award Winning
&
#1 International Bestselling Author
Jen Taylor, LCSW

ELITE PUBLISHING
HOUSE
YOUR LEGACY. YOUR BOOK.

First Edition
Copyright 2024 © Jen Taylor, LCSW
All Rights Reserved
No part of this book may be reproduced or transmitted in any form or by any means, electronic or mechanical, including photocopying, recording or by an information storage and retrieval system – except by a reviewer who may quote brief passages in a review to be printed in a magazine, newspaper or on the Web – without permission in writing from the publisher.
Cover Graphics: Kathryn Denhof

ELITE PUBLISHING HOUSE
YOUR LEGACY. YOUR BOOK.

To my dad, Dr. John William Traylor III

And my son, Giancarlo Taylor Fani, with love always

UNITED STATES:

AA: https://www.aa.org/find-aa

Debtors anonymous: 800-421-2383 – US Only

Underearners anonymous: https://www.underearnersanonymous.org/

Narcotics Anonymous: +1.818.773.9999

Al-Anon : 1-888-4AL-ANON (1-888-425-2666)

Gamblers anonymous: (909) 931-9056

Sexaholics Anonymous: +1 615-370-6062

Overeaters Anonymous: +1 505-891-2664

Workaholics Anonymous: (512) 415-8468

Caffeine Addicts Anonymous: info@caffeineaddictsanonymous.com

TABLE OF CONTENTS

FOREWORD 10

    Pia Marinangeli PhD LCSW CASAC

INTRODUCTION 12

COLLECTION OF LETTERS 16

    Jen Taylor

    Anonoymous

    Singha

    Beth Walker

    Gene Yonish

    Guinevere Smith

    Gene Yonish

    Lynsey Brown

    Anthony Chaparro

    Nicole Barker

    Blair Hayse

ADDITIONAL LETTERS TO MYSELF 84

    Dad

    Tonya Nichols, your bonus mom

MESSAGES OF HOPE *92*

APPENDIX ON SUPPORT RESOURCES *95*

APPENDIX ON SUICIDE RESOURCES *99*

   Includes Resources for Suicide Help & Assessment

CONDUCT A SUICIDE INQUIRY *112*

DETERMINE RISK LEVEL *115*

ABOUT THE AUTHOR *117*

Foreword

Pia Marinangeli PhD LCSW CASAC

Clinician, Presenter, Author, Mentor, and recent recipient of a Lifetime Achievement Award in Addiction Treatment

For the past 35 years as a psychotherapist, I have devoted my professional career to helping addicted persons and their loved ones. Addicts, in my opinion, are some of the most sensitive, loving, and kindest people on the planet, but have never learned to manage their feelings. In a world where we often seek comfort and relief from the pressures of daily life, the use of substances and subsequent potential addiction is a pervasive challenge that affects individuals from all walks of life. Addiction does not discriminate. It is a powerful force that can consume individuals and devastate families of all ages, socio-economic groups, and demographic areas.

Many people who become addicted to alcohol and other drugs also suffer from mental illness or emotional trauma. Initially, the drugs work well to help soothe painful feelings and troublesome thoughts. However, due to the nature of the substance and its impact on the brain, a tolerance is developed, and more and more substances are needed to have the same effect. Thus, the uncontrollable desire to obtain and use the substance at all costs.

In the past year alone, over 46 million Americans over the age of 12 have battled a substance use disorder. Surprisingly, less than 10 percent of these millions of people suffering ever receive treatment. The biggest barrier is shame and stigma. Addicted persons have been shunned, punished, and ostracized for decades. The way our society views addiction, often as a moral failure, is harmful to people who find themselves struggling to control their substance use. Many suffer alone and in silence, while others face harsh rejection and backlash from their family and friends. People become trapped in a vicious cycle of negative consequences in their work, relationships, and self-esteem, only to be ridiculed and judged by outsiders. This shame and stigma have prevented millions of people from seeking treatment. We must begin to look at substance use disorder through a new lens- not as a moral failing but as a chronic illness that must be treated with compassion, skill, and urgency.

Whether you are struggling with addiction yourself or supporting a loved one who is, this book is a must-read. Jen Taylor provides a forum for voices who have been in pain to share their strength, resilience, hope, and recovery. Their voices are inspiring and empowering. In this beautiful book, Jen sheds light on this often stigmatized issue and will hopefully provide the courage and support for someone to ask for help. There is hope for healing. It is possible to break free from the cycle of addiction and reclaim your life!

"Courage isn't having the strength to go on - it is going on when you have no strength"

- Napoleon Bonaparte

"I finally summoned up the courage to say the three words that would change my life: 'I need help.'"

- Elton John

Introduction

Addiction is a challenging topic. It often triggers us, either from some past experience or from a visceral reaction that society has fostered - often of disdain or judgment.

I have my own story of growing up in an alcoholic home. My father drank, mainly as a means to try to numb the pain he was feeling. He had suffered trauma from a very young age, including abandonment, the death of his mother at age 3, sexual abuse, being placed in an orphanage, Korea, and divorce. My mother was a working mom of 4, and it was nearly impossible for her to have room for empathy for her husband as she was busy keeping everything together. It felt like my father was often judged for his addiction rather than empathized with growing up. As I grew up and understood more, I didn't understand why he was not met with more understanding. Practically, I understood my mother was overwhelmed, but emotionally, I felt it was unfair that his illness was not treated as such. According to the Mayo Clinic, addiction is caused by the following: "Surges of dopamine in the reward system cause the reinforcement of pleasurable but unhealthy behaviors like taking drugs, leading people to repeat the behavior again and again. As a person continues to use drugs, the brain adapts by reducing the ability of cells in the reward circuit to respond to it."

Alcoholism is not understood as the illness that it is. If we were to consider addiction from the lens of illness, like diabetes or heart disease, life would be very different for those suffering from these illnesses.

An excerpt from Yale Medicine explains the addicted brain very well:
Addiction is now understood to be a brain disease. Whether it's alcohol, prescription pain pills, nicotine, gambling, or something else, overcoming an addiction isn't as simple as just stopping or exercising greater control over impulses.

That's because addiction develops when the pleasure circuits in the brain get overwhelmed, in a way that can become chronic and sometimes even permanent. This is what's at play when you hear about reward "systems" or "pathways" and the role of dopamine when it comes to addiction. But what does any of that really mean?

One of the most primitive parts of the brain, the reward system, developed as a way to reinforce behaviors we need to survive - such as eating. When we eat foods, the reward pathways activate a chemical called dopamine, which, in turn, releases a jolt of satisfaction. This encourages you to eat again in the future.

When a person develops an addiction to a substance, it's because the brain has started to change. This happens because addictive substances trigger an outsized response when they reach the brain. Instead of a simple, pleasurable surge of dopamine, many drugs of abuse - such as opioids, cocaine, or nicotine - cause dopamine to flood the reward pathway, ten times more than a natural reward.

The brain remembers this surge and associates it with the addictive substance. However, with chronic use of the substance, over time, the brain's circuits adapt and become less sensitive to dopamine. Achieving that pleasurable sensation becomes increasingly important, but at the same time, you build tolerance and need more and more of that substance to generate the level of high you crave.

Addiction can also cause problems with focus, memory, and learning, not to mention decision-making and judgment. Seeking drugs, therefore, is driven by habit - and not conscious, rational decisions.

I hope this book helps us alter our perspective on addiction and to have compassion for the individual with the addiction.

Thank you to those who have been vulnerable and shared your story.

Thank you to the reader for bearing witness.

Signs of an Overdose

If you know someone who uses drugs, particularly opioids or fentanyl, watch for these overdose symptoms:

- Cold, clammy skin
- Cyanosis
- Pinpoint Pupils
- Slowed respiration
- Unconsciousness*

If someone is sleeping or unconscious, move them into the recovery position.

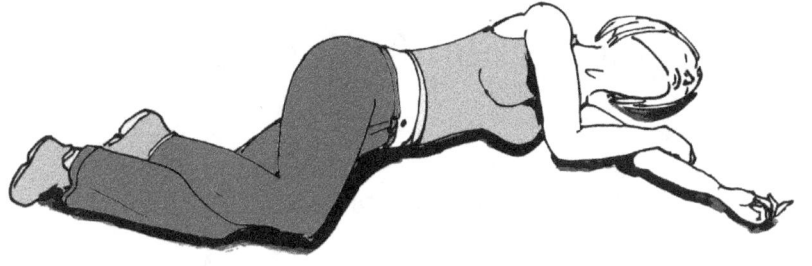

Recovery Position

After calling 911, place any unconscious person in the recovery position while you wait for help to arrive. This allows any bodily fluids to drain out of the mouth and nose, reducing the risk of aspiration and asphyxiation.

- Place the person on their side.
- Bend their knees (as in the fetal position).
- Rest their head on top of the arm closest to the floor.
- From The National Center for Drug Abuse Statistics

Collection Of Letters

Johnny Boy

I guess you could say that I lived a full life.
If I had taken better care of myself, I might have lived longer.

My only regret is for my daughter - we could have had more time together.

I moved to New York City in my early 20s to attend art school. My family thought I was studying at The Arts Students League. I did some modeling for a few different companies to make ends meet.

I was trying hard to get rid of my Alabama accent - it sounded dumb to me. My brother in Cali was a chicken farmer - it's not something to write home about.

I lost my momma when I was about three years old to TB. There were a bunch of us kids – maybe five. Charley was from another man. I don't know the details. Who knew how much my life would change after she died? My father didn't know or care to know what to do with us. He only cared about his bourbon and cigarettes. We ended up going to an orphanage. I found some love and support there. I guess I didn't really have a good example of how to parent. I was kind of on my own. My little brother looked up to me like a dad. I'm afraid I disappointed him. I did my best, but I was only a few years older than him. I don't think he ever learned to read and write.

My father was an alcoholic – one of the mean kind. The kind that yelled and made us do things to him - things he should never have asked his children to do. I never told anyone this until I was about 60. I was so ashamed. But with therapy, I realized it wasn't my fault – this was his fault, and he was most likely abused by someone, too. The sexual abuse affected my sleep and my eating. Sometimes I couldn't eat at all. I would try to have something soft, like a banana or a smoothie. I always had nightmares - even before Korea. The night didn't feel safe for me.

On my way to Basic Training, I kept thinking this must be some kind of mistake - my father would get me out of it, and I'd be able to go home. But I ended up in battle - I saw my best friend killed in front of me. I killed, so I didn't get killed. I'm not sure why I thought my father would be there for me. He never was. He was only there when he needed something from me. I tried to protect my sister, but I think he eventually got us all.
I always felt I had to "look good" and "keep up appearances." For as long as I can remember, no one ever asked how Johnny felt inside. So, I hid my inside parts, smiled, dressed well, and hoped no one would notice. R & R in the Army meant drinking and smoking cigarettes. Drinking became my solace - a place to drift away into a numbing, floaty feeling where the memories of what he did faded and my self-hatred and disgust were muted.

Despite the abuse and the trauma of losing my momma so young, I think I did ok. I was a special education teacher and have been married a few times. I had a kid - she's telling my story. I loved the best I could, the best I knew how. I'm not sure it was enough for the kids, but I sincerely tried my best. I tried many times to give up drinking, but the problem was I was doing it for someone else - my kids, my wife, and never me. I guess I felt too vulnerable. I never felt strong enough to survive without that protection from the outside world or my inside world.

So, my suggestion is – do it for you. You are worth it. Give up the alcohol, the pills. Get help. You are worth it. Learn from my mistakes.

- Jen Taylor

As obvious as it may sound, nobody expects to be an addict. A lot of things I remember saying when I was a younger teen were in total retaliation against drugs or something along the lines of, "Oh, I would never do that." Looking back, it's really funny to think I would threaten to end friendships over people smoking weed "too much" without knowing in just a couple of years, I would start doing harder drugs than the majority of the friends I've had. I didn't realize that young me just wanted to escape reality. I struggled to keep my mind at bay, constantly anxious with every thought, continually stressed with every decision/action, or, more often, lacked decision/action. On top of my mental state being a constant mess, I was also sick often during these times. Being older made me realize a lot of my physical health was correlated with how much my mental health was suffering. That is where the story of addiction starts.

Rather innocently. At 12, I had a glass of champagne. No harm, no cravings for more. At 14, during the summer going into my first year of high school, I smoked weed for the first time. Once again, no harm, no cravings. As I went into high school, a lot of friends started smoking weed way more often. That was concerning to me, as I would only smoke 1-2 times a week at the most. Although my drug addiction would start soon, my original addiction was video games. That was my escape, and it worked up until there was no joy in games without substance attached. From what I remember, up until about 16 years old, everything was still very casual, and substances were still a non-issue. The first time I remember wanting more was when I took my first Vyvanse. Vyvanse is another form of Adderall.

My friend was getting one for himself, and the guy selling it asked if I wanted to try one. We were all hanging out, and I figured, "Why not? Realistically, what is the worst thing this can do to me?" It shifted the path of my life to an extent. It can sound so silly to someone who hasn't experienced addiction.

"How can one silly pill change so much?"

"Why didn't you stop once you realized it would become an addiction?"

Both are fair questions that I still don't fully know the answers to. The feeling I got completely flushed away my anxiety, as well as the voice in my head that told me what I had to say, didn't matter. Between the euphoria and the subtraction of my negative thoughts, I was truly in bliss for that night. Soon after that night, I reached out for more. It was only $5 per pill, it was strong (50 MG), and it lasted about 8 hours. I found myself being up all night (as it is a stimulant), playing games, smoking weed when I could sneak it, and feeling great. I had also picked up vaping at this time, which, to this day, I haven't kicked.

I hadn't smoked too consistently up to this point. Once I met my ex at 17, just a couple of months after taking my first pill, is when I started to smoke practically every single day, which turned to multiple times a day. By the time we met, I was already hooked on Adderall. I was taking it most days. A little into our dating, I decided to get a prescription for Adderall. This way, I wouldn't have to wait for the seller to be available, and I'd be getting way more for way less money. My seventeenth year in this world was when addiction would forever change my life.

I had insomnia prior to this point. The Adderall made it worse. The abuse of Adderall made it WAY worse. For this, I was prescribed Ambien. I had already had the Ambien but wasn't using it. It was "as needed," and I cared more about being awake and feeling high rather than being asleep. To me, sleeping was missing out on life. My mentality had changed when I realized Ambien also made me feel good, possibly better. Instead of fighting the anxiety and bad thoughts, like Adderall had been doing, it helped me completely disassociate. I had no idea that was what I had wanted until it happened. Pure peace, no thoughts, no worries, no nothing. My show and my mind floating around. When I did have thoughts on Ambien, they were always loving. I would smother my girlfriend with thoughtful and loving texts while high on it, reaching out to people I had lost touch with. It made me want to show appreciation those few times I wasn't in my "zone" of disassociation.

I've spoken a lot about my use but not of the consequences it had on my relationships. That's because it hadn't until now. In my experience, the weight that addiction has on your loved ones and your relationships with them is way worse than the effect it has on you. It's one thing to be a detriment to your own health, at your expense, with your funds. Way more pain comes when it starts having a negative impact on those who care about you. It has these effects on everyone and everything you do. You don't act as you once did. The addiction takes over who you are and what you prioritize. When you argue, you don't argue from your morals and values; you argue in defense of the addictions' morals and values. When you put yourself first selfishly over someone you claim to love unconditionally, it doesn't mean you are selfish at heart; the addiction is. I don't think everyone gets that. It's also ironic because, in the treatment, they say, "You are not your addiction." I think that's what I'm trying to say, though. You become your addiction while in it, and it can be terrifying. If you shed the addiction or don't let it control your life, then you get who you truly are at heart.

The first time this showed was just a couple of months into my girlfriend and I dating. Throughout the entire day, I felt anxious and irritable. I don't remember the reason, but it isn't very surprising to have days like that when you are taking several substances throughout each day. I had no idea of the interactions some medications may have, even though I'm confident that my psychiatrist at the time told me that there were dangerous ones with Ambien and Adderall. I had known that someone in my house took something for anxiety, and I decided to help myself to a few. At the time, I didn't realize this was a benzodiazepine, similar to Xanax. I kept taking more as time went on due to the fact that my anxiety had not subsided yet. Just a little later, my girlfriend and best friend came over. Soon after their arrival, I blacked out. The next thing I remembered clearly was being in the hospital. I am very irritated and overall confused. I spoke to my mom, who was clearly worried sick about what had transpired. Having no recollection of the events, she explains them to me. I don't remember how I reacted then, but I realized I was disappointed. I had completely gone off on my girlfriend for seemingly nothing important. I then lashed out at my friend, who was trying to calm me down. I ended up kicking them both out and locked myself in my room. I had hurt everyone in that situation, all of whom I love so much.

Nothing changed

I kept taking the things I could access and trying things when they crossed my path.

Skipping far ahead to when I was 19. Addiction was already deeply rooted into me. Unknowingly, I hadn't gotten addicted to my drugs of choice yet (drugs of choice, meaning the drugs that led to me getting to such a low point that I had no other option in my mind besides getting help). I and that ex I mentioned dated for another two or so years before taking a break. I had stopped taking Adderall at this point as I was more about the downers at this point. It sort of faded out as I found what I liked more in being high. Right before that break, we started to indulge in other drugs together—acid, cocaine, Percocet, Xanax, etc. Xanax was something different for me. That was not real Xanax, though. We got it from one of our dealers on Snapchat. Snapchat had little to no regulation on selling drugs at that time. People would just post the product and prices onto their story; you'd swipe up, tell them what you want, and meet up. Who knows what else was in this besides alprazolam (Xanax), but it felt like nothing I'd ever experienced prior. It makes a lot of sense in hindsight that this drug would make me feel the best. There was so much anxiety, second-guessing, paranoia, and being undiagnosed bipolar at the time as well. Simply, it just numbed all the things that needed to be numbed. Timelines and months become a lot clearer at this point. Having found Xanax at 19, I was just coming off 20 when the break had started. My good childhood friend and I also reconnected during this time. That was at the end of summer, and we planned not to talk until December of that year because we had already planned to go to a concert together.

Those few months following the break mainly consisted of me and this friend getting high on Xanax and weed most nights. At some point, I had gotten a prescription, but since I was abusing it, once I ran out for the month, I would get more from the street. Considering that it was cut with so much other bullshit, I was in its clutches. So was my best friend. We would watch each other "zombie out" every night. We even watched each other almost die a couple of times… but did we stop? Nah. To us, it was fun—no such thing as answering a wake-up call in those times. God had given me many wake-up calls during that time. Not even entirely due to the drug use. Once my ex and I reunited, we were just different people. It lasted about a month until we entirely called it quits. Our breakup was a long time coming, and I had already had my eyes on someone else at this point. Honestly, the old relationship and the one I was pursuing were probably doomed from the start.

Fast forward to March 2020. I had been trying to find myself again after such a long relationship when Covid hit the world. Still deep in my addiction and with no one to see outside of my immediate family, I turned to drugs for comfort, especially for those first five months or so. I was seeking out products where I could. I got a bottle of almost 90 Adderall to pass the time, some Xanax, and a shit ton of alcohol. I never was much of a drinker before quarantine. Maybe a few beers here and there. When introducing my second drug of choice, alcohol, which, in tandem with my other favorite drug, is an overdose waiting to happen, mixing different pills and substances was something that I had done frequently, but not like this. I stopped answering my phone, ignored everyone, and just isolated myself. My friends and I would get together once the restrictions were a little looser. I must have hidden it well because those who I didn't want to know what I was taking didn't. But oh, how obvious it was to those who knew. There wasn't a single gathering that I hadn't used for.

A little into the fall of 2020, I finally ended up having an overdose. I probably wouldn't be here today if it weren't for my best friend. I started seeing this girl I had reconnected with recently. She didn't know about my Xanax use. I hid it from her, knowing she was a lot more put together than my previous girlfriend, at least in the sense of substance abuse and emotional understanding. I cared about her, but I preferred being alone. I was making my way home from her house early that night to get a 1.5-liter bottle of wine after already drinking one while at hers and some Xanax from my plug.

I opened the wine, washed the Xanax down, went for a walk, and met up with my friend. I remember meeting with him four blocks from my house and then nothing but darkness. Years after my prior incident, I woke up in the hospital again. This time was different, though; it was serious. I had no gratitude to give, though, only hate, because when I got home, I found the rest of my pills missing. I knew this was not my friend stealing them, but instead trying to save me from them. He had just saved me from dying, and I called him, screaming to give my pills back to me. I threatened him in every way I could. He never gave in. He took it on the chin, cried, and tried to get me to understand that he didn't want to see his best friend die. Seeing how different I am today compared to that time in my life is insane. There were so many more incidents and arguments through the years—a bunch of missed events or obligations that let family and friends down. If not missing them, then showing up to them and making a fool of myself. These dark times eventually led to a suicide attempt that winter. I kept spiraling more and more and was doing little to stop myself from falling deeper into a hole.

In April of 2021, that girlfriend dumped me. I had disappointed her more than too many times in our little time together. Though it was mainly for her, she also told me she did it out of care as well, knowing I'd never get myself out of that place with her being my crutch. I had to heal and change on my own. I'm glad she had the self-respect to do so because it ended up leading me to try and become fully sober for the first time in many years. To this day, that was my rock bottom. I wasn't working, I was no longer in school, I lost many friends due to isolation and lack of care, and I was addicted to numerous substances. I couldn't take it anymore and asked my parents and friends for a solution.

Not only did I need help handling life and fixing the mentality I had, but firstly and most importantly, I knew I needed to stop taking drugs. I decided to cut it all out: the nightly beers, my Xanax, my Ambien, and the weed. I had quit nicotine at this point for a few months. It may have been ill-advised to start the detox alone and without tapering, but I was done. I couldn't give up that momentum. The fact that I actually wanted to be sober had to be a sign because I couldn't remember the last time I was voluntarily sober before that. I couldn't sleep or eat for days. On the best of days, I'd eat a couple of bites and sleep for maybe 40 minutes. The nausea and chills were more common than not, and the mental anguish was indescribable. I couldn't take it after those few days. I turned to my mom for a solution; she knew me and understood my history well.

Michael, a recently deceased family friend of ours, had told us about a place in Los Angeles that past summer when I was going through another incident with Xanax. The thought of my parents spending any money on me due to my own poor decisions hurt to think about, but that was a way better option than the road I was going down. Within a few hours of the idea being brought up by my mom, we called the treatment center and inquired about details and financial options. We discovered I could go at a significantly lower price, a little under 10% of the original monthly cost. I was scared as hell, but the call gave me hope. The idea grew on me quickly. I discussed it with friends, and they thought it would be perfect for me if it were financially viable. No more than a day later, I made the decision to do my intake, book the flight, and get the help I needed. Every hour still felt like hell, but knowing soon I would be safe and with guidance gave me more peace of mind than I had felt recently.

April 21st 2021, I changed my life. I landed in Los Angeles and was driven to the detox center before I could go to the actual rehabilitation area. The detox had almost been done before I even arrived, but that first night there, I was able to eat and sleep so well. It felt so freeing knowing that I was in good hands and I was taking the steps to get better. They took my phone, which made me anxious at first, but I later realized having my phone caused way more anxiety than not having it. A few days later, I drove to the treatment center and started my journey to healing.

Being in LA for those three months completely changed the trajectory of my life. Before going in, I had no hope and entirely lost myself. Coming back to NYC, I spoke like myself again; I felt like me again; I learned so many things about how to overcome my mentalities and why parts of me are this way. I was 90 days sober.

Then I drank. Here's the thing about that. I don't regret it. I felt so much guilt for relapsing, but the thing is, when I had gone into treatment, I had no intention of being fully sober. I had the intention to stop the hard stuff and to be able to limit my intake of the lesser things that were not necessarily deadly in moderation. The main thing that I don't regret breaking my sobriety is because, during those three months, I healed and found myself, so much so that three years later, in 2024, I am the happiest and healthiest I have ever been in my 24 years on this earth.]

Am I fully sober? Absolutely not. Am I striving more than I have ever strived before? Yes, I am. It may not seem like much to others, but I have been working nonstop since returning. I have been taking care of my mental and physical well-being. I have been a better son, brother, friend, acquaintance, coworker, and an overall better person. My relationships with those I care about are stronger than they have been in many years. My mind is at ease, without substances playing a role. I choose when I want to smoke or drink recreationally occasionally. The addiction does not tell me to have constant substances.

I took my life back from addiction. I WAS ME AGAIN. I AM ME AGAIN. A new me, not my addiction, not anymore. Some people don't want help, some have a tough time getting help, and some have no support system to let them see they need help. No matter how hard it is, seek a way to get help. Addiction is life or death. It is quite literally a toss of the dice on your life. Any drug in excess can and will kill you. It's all a matter of when. I was in denial and had to reach the absolute darkest point in my life up to this point just to think of getting help.

Thank God, I did. I may not be here today if I hadn't made that choice to save myself. I beg that you consider seeking the help you need if you are struggling similarly. There is always hope yet, and you are important. If you think you aren't, you're important to me. I don't care that I don't know you. I care about you. I've been there, and I don't wish it upon anyone. Your addiction never defines you. You are not your addiction. You deserve better. You Are better. Allow yourself to heal and find the real you. Your future self will thank you.

- Anonymous

Namaskar.

I am Singha, and I am 33 now.

My story is all about becoming a spiritual person from an alcohol addict. It was 2012 when I was 22 years old; up until then, I was fully addicted. I had some traumas as a child, and the issues with my family broke me from the inside. I started drinking when I was 18. I remember that day when I met my spiritual teacher, December 12th, 2012. After our very first meeting, my spiritual teacher realized that I was deeply addicted to alcohol.

As a child, I was so frustrated and depressed because my parents treated me as an unwanted child, and they never accepted me. They always loved my elder brother and gave him all the attention. As a result, my childhood was destroyed, and during my teen years, I became an alcoholic. I used to complain about my life all the time, but now I have realized that it was all a lesson and that I needed to stand up firm in the face of my problems.

He requested that I join his ashram and practice yoga and meditation. Initially, it was like hell for me; my urge was so high that I used to run away from the ashram, and at the same time, I was fighting from the inside to become clean of this addiction.

After a few weeks, yoga and meditation started showing results. I became a vegetarian - that also helped a lot. After six months of practicing yoga and meditation, I completely came out from the addiction to alcohol, and I realized that forgiveness is the cure for all trauma. Forgive those who have mistreated you, for love brings love, and hate brings hate. I don't blame my parents. I am thankful that they gave birth to me. Thanks to them, I can see the beautiful world and all beautiful things as a human being. Sometimes, we need to understand that our parents are humans and have made their own parenting mistakes. It may be that they had their own difficult childhoods. I am not defending child abuse by parents. I am only saying that they are also human and can make mistakes.

It may sound very easy, but it was a tough battle and such a hard time for me. I believe we must see ourselves in the mirror once a day and ask ourselves what we are doing with the life God or Mother Nature gave us without taking anything in return. As human beings, we must realize that we have to live our lives with purity and happiness. When our actions and activities make our family and friends happy, it makes our lives successful, and it also makes us happy and prosperous. I feel it's just about our minds. We are strong enough to fight our urges - we just need to be who we are, and nothing is more precious than our lives, which affects everyone around us.

Thanks for allowing me to share my story.

- Singha

Dear Future Me,

Maybe I should start this "DEAR ME!" It feels more like an expletive situation than not. I am sitting here with a soda right by me. Don't worry, it is diet. Actually, worry. I just came from the doctor, and she is now concerned about our kidneys. That woman never says anything positive. If she only knew how difficult things were, she might have a little pity for us.

Remember the first time we tried to give up sugared soda drinks? We didn't make it to the end of the day. That was before we had incentive. We knew they were not good for us. Every time we would start down a health trip, we would attempt to give them up. Over and over, we would attempt to give them up. First, the headaches would start. The pain that felt like the eyes were going to burst out of the skull and hang by their optic nerves. It would quickly spread into the whole brain, migrating down the brain stem into the spine. It was steady, too. There was no relief until we took that sweet poison back into our system. If we did not, the stomach aches would start. Being nauseated was probably from the headache. Sometimes, vomiting was the only way to find relief. After that, the feeling of anger and agitation began. Everything annoyed us. People would start desperately avoiding us. Eventually, some friend or loved one would throw a soda at us. "Just drink it!" They would say.

We gave up cigarettes and alcohol so fast. It was hardly an effort. But sugared cold drinks? Hell no. When I think of a person with an addiction, I think of drugs. I think of poor old alcoholics sitting in dirty alleys. I think of opium dens. Not carbonation. I would never have called us an addict back then. We had a serious problem, though. It was just a sociably acceptable problem.

Then, the day came when that problem caught up to us. Remember sitting in that sterile office, looking down at the parking lot, waiting for blood work? We had been in a car accident. The doctor informed us that we needed to be in a hospital. That shock still echoes in me today when I think about it. The feeling of just *WHAT?!* We found out that day we had diabetes. Our sugar level was way high. Remember how we walked out to the parking lot feeling lost and scared? Remember not going to the hospital - hahaha. That was never going to happen. It was the holidays, for crying out loud. The denial had begun.

In the end, remembering our grandfather made us take action. He lost his legs one piece at a time because of diabetes. He lost pieces of himself bit by bit until he finally mercifully died.

We got the carbs under control. We knocked out eating candy, cakes, and cookies. It was easy enough. We just repeated to ourselves, "I like having toes." The sugared sodas, though, were another matter. It was almost like if we didn't have them, we became evil, demonic, twisted, and angry. Even people who wanted us to live sugar-free would be like, "Here, just drink one. Please! I will buy it for you." We tried to switch to diet, but it was just not the same. Those sugared sodas did something for us that was unmatched by anything else. It was a kick of energy and happiness. We didn't even have to eat if we had those sugared drinks. That led to reasoning with ourselves. We were doing better by staying on them. We were happy, and we ate less. Excuses!

The dreaded blood work broke those illusions fast. The sugar never went down. We finally had to face the facts. We had to let go of the one thing that made us happy.

The first week was hell. No medicine helped with the headaches. The feeling of being sick and throwing up was even worse. No one would believe what we went through. Our mood? It was like someone fed us after midnight! We yelled at everyone. People started avoiding us! We would look at all the bad things that could happen being diabetic. It helped motivate us to push past the pain. Still, it almost seemed worth it just to have one.

The sugar-free didn't have the same effect. We learned to like it. It helped a little. It took a month or more to finally be okay with not having a sugared soda. We finally managed it. If I am honest with you, I still want one when things are bad in life. I never take one. Never. I know if I get one sip, I will go back to them.

Later, we would find out about all our vitamin deficiencies. Sometimes, when a person has a food addiction, it is because they are unable to process specific vitamins. In this case, it was iron, vitamin D, and B. The energy I felt from the sugared soda replaced the energy I missed from not having these vitamins. For us, that was part of the problem. For us, the problem was also part of the cause. Sugared sodas filled us up, taking away our need to eat, which led to a lack of vitamins, which led to needing more sugared sodas.

A simple blood test helped to find out what we needed. Once we had that information, we took prescribed supplements and shots. At some points, we even had to have infusions. A few times, we needed blood transfusions. The addiction to sugared sodas had covered up an underlying condition. We had iron-deficient anemia as well as pernicious anemia. We also had very little vitamin D. Once we began replacing these vital things, it was easier to let go of the sugared sodas.

The mental pleasure we got from drinking the sodas had to be dealt with, too. We loved sipping iced cold carbonated drinks while we read a book. It helped us relax. It calmed us down when things were horrible. Luckily, after the vitamin fix, switching to diet sodas was easier.

Now, our kidneys are not behaving. Diabetes is a harsh taskmaster. Now, we face giving up even sugar-free sodas. I am thinking of starting a Soda Anonymous. Honestly, who would come? It is such a silly thing to be addicted to. It is such a silly thing to let control your life. It does! If we let it. It will control our lives until it kills us. It is, at the end of the day, an addiction. Even now, knowing I need to let them go, I have one sitting by me. Sipping that sweet, acidic nectar brings me peace of mind while I write this.

Dear self, dear me, dear future me, please, please don't let it control us. We kicked cigarettes, alcohol, cakes, cookies, and lots of other things. We even kicked sugared sodas. We can kick this.

Now, I am going to get a glass of water and pretend I don't want a soda.

Sincerely, Yourself

- Beth Walker

Diet Coke Addiction
written by: Gene Yonish

It started in 1998,

At Roosevelt Field Mall, New York State.

It started with just one,

And an idle mind.

I sought to unwind,

And have some fun.

"Little did I know,"

How the numbers would exponentially grow.

Do I honestly enjoy,

Treating my mind like a toy?

Deceit-

Another self-control defeat.

I "can't take the heat."

My drug,

Is actually Diet Coke.

This ain't no joke.

Caffeine might not be sold by thugs,

But it is very controlling,

And it can affect my brain,

Where my cognitive abilities can be slowing.

Is it worth the pain?

Is there anything to gain?

No!

This insanity must go.

All the dough,

Foolishly spent.

Even delayed paying of my rent.

How can I terminate,

My misguided ways?

Wait!

I need to listen to the Director of the play.

What does God say?

Life is more than what I drink or eat.

I can beat,

This,

Before I piss,

My life away.

What else can I say?

God, help me.

I'm down on my knees.

Please,

Take away the attraction to the taste.

Help me to see how my life is becoming a
   waste.

The end result can be well-being.

My faith in Jesus is the only long-term solution
   worth seeing.

Now, I must put into practice what I believe.

Diet Coke- get out of my life- LEAVE!!

- Gene Yonish

I have had many different relationships with food. I can even date it back to when I was ten years old and in the fourth grade. As I get older and get to know myself, I am fully aware I have a toxic relationship with food. I wish with my whole soul that it was just something I used for nourishment. I suppose there are small time frames that I managed that healthy balance. However, to be frank, this addiction is highly encouraged, warped, and easily disguised. It's not illegal, very affordable to maintain, and easy to function around. Of course, I have a joke that no ice cream or chocolate can be left in the house, or it torments me until it is gone. Talk about addiction. I don't keep it in the house for emotional support anymore. My children even have a joke….. mom, please don't eat that (insert yummy guilty food) in the night!?

I have done a ton of reflecting on my toxic relationships with my food over the years. I can remember it dating back to as early as ten years old. I asked my mom why, when I get overwhelmed with school work and projects, I have to eat to prepare to tackle them. I wish my mom had zoned in on her own eating habits and had healed whatever that was because she just told me that was pretty normal. Maybe for her, but it's not healthy. In the end, I genuinely believe the unhealed part of her life provided her a slow death, and that was in part due to her food addiction.

Food can either heal us or harm us. I don't believe there is an in-between. For example, so many food sensitivities affect our brains, organs, joints, gut, and mental health. If you are not paying attention, those foods damage any weak link in our system.

In hindsight, the subsequent realization was in my 30s. I was a mom of three kids and exhausted. I started to observe I would binge eat when I was tired. I was all the time but once I slowed down and just should have gone to bed, I would eat. I probably rationalized that I had not eaten all day and that it was quiet in the house after the kids went to bed so I could get some things done from my to-do list. Not to mention the sugar rush needed to get things done. I am grateful for this awareness so I can discern my evenings.

From around my mid-30s, I started playing around with all of the diets… gluten-free, paleo, carb-free, vegetarian, and vegan. Some very extremes, to say the least. It is where I discovered a lot of my food sensitivities. There have been a lot of times I wished I could just drink water and take supplements. Then, I wouldn't be tempted by my drug. However, through all of these processes of different diets and ruling out allergens and sensitivities, it allowed me to see my addiction to food at its finest (Insert eye roll here). That would ALWAYS highlight my addiction habits, especially when I was diagnosed with type II diabetes. It's just another way food is attacking my body.

Through several awareness practices and the hard truth, I have adopted some healthy ways to cope. That does not mean I'm on point 100% of the time. I can recognize when I disregard my awareness and get some chocolate-covered pretzels.

Food addiction is fully adaptable and accepted in an unhealthy culture like ours. Self-love is the only thing that has helped me keep it at bay. I have to love myself and eat what my body needs. Nobody else can motivate me with that. It's a hard road, but I will continue to do what I can to learn and grow to be the best version of myself for my family and my goals. You can too.

- Guinevere Smith

The Battle of Sex

written by Gene Yonish

Sex is so much fun.

If I were a woman, I'd never make it as a nun.

My thoughts in filthy places.

As if I continually want to run all the bases.

I treat sex like a drug.

I always want my fix.

It messes with my sensitive mind.

A way to unwind.

My thoughts are sick.

I hope that the authorities don't need to post my mug.

What is the cure,

For this whore?

"Flee from temptation,"

Before I'm a target of a police investigation.

Am I being too hard on me?

Do I need to show myself more grace?

Going to the same places,

Expecting different results- insanity!

Distractions can be of aide,

Until the obsession fades,

Away.

Call an accountability man,

And pray.

Have a battle plan.

I can win this one,

Only with my reliance in God's Son.

- Gene Yonish

Losing my mother to cancer when I was only four years old marked the beginning of a tumultuous journey through life. In my formative years, I grappled with academic challenges that left me feeling inadequate and unprepared for the world beyond the classroom. This struggle, coupled with a sense of uncertainty and lack of direction, led me to seek solace in alcohol at the tender age of 12. As I navigated through my teenage years, my confidence in my abilities dwindled, and the notion that success was reserved for those who pursued higher education became deeply ingrained in my subconscious.

As I stepped into adulthood, my conviction that success hinged on obtaining a university degree led to a cycle of self-fulfilling prophecy. I became convinced that without higher education, I was destined for mediocrity, propelling me further into a path of self-destruction. Eventually, I found myself ensnared in the grips of heroin addiction, a daunting abyss from which escape felt impossible. Through this struggle, I came to grasp the profound impact of subconscious beliefs formed in childhood and reinforced through repeated experiences. These beliefs mold our perceptions, expectations, and actions, ultimately determining the outcomes we attract into our lives.

I once thought my energy was overwhelming, feeling I was too much for others to handle. Yet, I've since embraced my vibrant energy, seeing it as a wellspring of strength and vitality that allows me to express myself fully and positively impact those around me. Through introspection and self-reflection, I've untangled the limiting beliefs that once held me back. I now comprehend the profound influence of both the conscious and subconscious mind in shaping our reality.

As I began to cultivate a newfound sense of self-belief, I witnessed a profound shift in my reality. Doors that once seemed firmly shut began to swing open, revealing endless possibilities and opportunities for growth. I realized that external circumstances or societal expectations do not predetermine success but are instead a reflection of our own belief in ourselves and our ability to persevere in the face of adversity.

Today, as a keynote speaker and mentor, I serve as a living testament to the profound truth that the ability to transform our lives resides within each and every one of us. By deliberately utilizing our subconscious and conscious minds, we unlock the incredible potential to rewrite the narratives of our existence, redefine the boundaries of our capabilities, and actualize our most fervent aspirations.

In addition to my speaking engagements and mentoring endeavors, I also channel my passion for growth and resilience into the realm of athletics. As a master athlete, proudly representing Ireland in sprints and hurdles, I embody the principles of determination and perseverance on the track, inspiring others to pursue their own athletic and personal goals with unwavering dedication.

Through unwavering self-belief and an unyielding dedication to personal evolution, we transcend the constraints of our circumstances, propelling ourselves towards achievements that surpass even our wildest imaginations.

- Lynsey Brown

Brown Magic

My eyes open. It's blurry for a second, and then I see it. An exhausted sigh of frustration whistles its way out from between my dry, cracked lips as I see that same water stain on the ceiling above me come into focus. Did the helpless 90-whatever-year-old lady upstairs drop another cup of coffee on the floor? Did she leave the faucet running in the kitchen sink again? Or did it finally happen? Is it a bloodstain from her head bouncing off the floor as her decrepit old limbs gave out after at least a century-long fight against gravity holding her weight? "Lucky," I think to myself enviously. My sore bones and muscles feel like they're screaming for relief as I force myself to sit up on the creaky pull-out sofa bed.

I'm still here.

The rest of the scene enters my vision: empty Arizona cans, torn open bags of ramen noodles, and college-ruled notebooks half-filled with the lyrics of the next big hit I wrote to change the world. My life is a twisted, depressed version of Groundhog Day.

I look down at my bony, malnourished forearm and the crumpled-up piece of paper in my lap. I am covered in leftover powdered remnants of the bag I managed to swindle the night before with some clever excuse and a promise of an IOU.

How am I not dead yet?!

I'm still here. Still living, still breathing, still wishing this poison would kill me already.

"I'm still here" meant another failed attempt at escape, another unanswered prayer. It's just a matter of time before I feel that 50-

pound rock in my gut, the aches in my legs, cold sweats, and the rest of the ever-present heroin withdrawal symptoms that have become my constant companion. I spend every day in agony, hunting a drug that my body craves in order to make it stop, yet it's the very drug that causes all of my physical and mental pain in the first place.

With tears in my eyes and snot dribbling off of my lips, I beg God to grant me one wish, like God is some omnipotent magical genie: "Please, let me go sleep and never wake up!"

But, goddammit, I'm still here. All that matters now, and what's mattered in the last four months, is my greed and desperation to make a bag of dope appear no matter what it takes- busking, selling, or stealing- to make my pain go away, at least momentarily.

I'm a stubborn and selfish Capricorn from Boston, half Irish and Venezuelan. I thought I knew a lot, and good luck to anyone who tried to convince me otherwise. I knew I was still here. Little did I know that I did not have all of the answers and that I would hit actual rock bottom in my very immediate future.

My plan today is the same as it's been for the last four months: get something in my stomach to stop the aches and pains, and then figure out a way to have money tomorrow to do it all again. I'm stalled in front of a convenience store in Malden Square. I stepped out of the GMC Yukon that I stole three days prior, which I later found out belonged to an off-duty Lynn police officer. What a great choice; of course, the first car I ever stole just happened to belong to a cop. It's part of a long list of bad decisions I've been making since, well...long before high school, now that I think about it.

I walk into the store unmasked, wary of the decision I'm about to make from the get-go. I scan the numerous shelves full of candy bars, chips, and midnight snacks. "I really don't want to do this" loops over and over in my head, mixed with multiple other outcomes of what will happen if I don't. "I can't do it," I think. I walk out of the store empty-handed. I'm back at square one. Broke, hungry, dope sick, short of rent money to send my son, and had no money in my pocket.

How did I get here? I was an A and B student in high school. I graduated, and I've been working since I was 12 years old. I never would have imagined in a million years that I'd be here at 33 years old. "I don't have a choice," I think to myself as I walk back into the store with a syringe exposed and demand that the cashier empty the register. I can feel the terror in her eyes as I hold up the needle. I'm equally terrified. I don't know how this works, and I just want the money and an easy exit. Eventually, I get what I want. I run down multiple side streets as I hear screams and cries for help coming from the corner store. I run in a zigzag path towards a friend's house who's also awaiting a quick payday to curb his symptoms. The deed is done, the money spent, and I finally feel normal again.

After about three weeks of hiding out, I got bored and decided to venture back out into the public. This goes against every intuition I had been feeling for the past month, and for good reason. As I walk back home, I'm approached by two officers in plain clothes who ask me if my name is Anthony. Why bother trying to lie my way out of it? They knew what I'd done, and I didn't have much left to lose at this point anyway. They take me to the station, I give my statement, and the details are enough to charge me and send me to my first day at Middlesex House of Correction and Jail in Billerica, Massachusetts. I'd be foolish to say I wasn't nervous, scared for my life, and remorseful of the actions I chose that got me to this situation. After an hour or so of intake procedures, I finally make my way to "the block." I hear shouts of "That's him!" and "I'll see you soon, son!" as I try to locate the cell number the correctional officer had just read to me. My cell door cracks open, and I step in to greet the obviously agitated cellmate I would spend the next God knows how many months or years with.

It's now two weeks into my first jail bid. I'm getting used to the routine, and the toxins are out of my system. I'm fully clean of any and all drugs, even cigarettes, for the first time since I was 11 years old. I'm even working out again. My cellmate found out I could rap and spread the word throughout the entire pod; now, I can't pass a single cell during rec time without being stopped and asked to freestyle for someone. I've also been reading books. I think I ended up reading more in jail than in my entire educational career. When you're on a 21-hour lockdown, there's nothing but time on your hands; you can either use that time to be productive or go crazy. I chose to fill it with writing, reading, working out, learning chess, self-reflection, and, most importantly, prayer. I finally accepted God into my life fully and began filling my prayers with gratitude rather than request. The change happened almost immediately. I was getting gifts from other inmates, such as extra meal trays, milk, and magazines. I even got good news on my case. I might actually be getting out of here soon.

The judge is giving me a chance. My prayers for an opportunity have been answered. The bailiff removes my wrist and ankle shackles to instead fit me with an ankle bracelet to track my every movement in my new residence. On the way, my mother informs me that one of my first childhood friends has committed suicide. Great, just when I was finding gratitude in all the small things in life that I've been ungrateful for. I hug my mother and make my way into this new place; It wasn't exactly a jail cell, but I wasn't exactly free either. I give a clean urine sample. It feels good, to some extent. There's a TV, basketball hoop, real food, and smoke breaks. I guess this is the law's way of slowly integrating you back into society. Baby steps.

The cycle begins. Program, relapse, homelessness, rehab, program, jail. The more I looked around, the more these faces and procedures felt like an expected consequence of my first offense. I always felt that people saying the "system" just wants to keep you as a statistic were simply unable to learn from their mistakes. "Stop committing crimes," I always thought. "Stop getting caught." But I was ignorant and inexperienced. Thinking there's some elaborate scheme to keep addicts in an endless cycle of jail and rehabilitation programs might just be my conspiracy mind at work, but I have to admit, there seems to be a lot more focus on rules for us to follow to be accepted as normal citizens rather than what could make us successful human beings in life. This was going to take more work than just following the rules and going to meetings. I would have to be my own advocate, social worker, therapist, sponsor, counselor, and probation officer. I had to hold myself accountable because, beyond the laws of this single residential program full of 20-plus other recovering addicts, no one else would. It worked for a good six months until I started working again, had more freedom, and stopped regularly going to church and meetings. I started slipping back into my old behaviors. Sure enough, I inevitably relapsed, got kicked out of the program, and was back in jail.

My lawyer explained to the judge that relapse, although frowned upon, was a common occurrence in early sobriety. I have to say that for the first time in my life of trying to get sober, six months wasn't a bad start. For the next three years, the cycle of programs, relapse, homelessness, jail, and detox seemed like it was destined to be my life until I just ended up as another statistic: dead from an overdose or spending the next 10 to 15 years behind bars. Needless to say, my faith in the system was shaken. Being able to see a light at the end of the tunnel was getting harder and harder, similar to the initial feelings I had in active addiction.

But, I was too determined to be a statistic. I had a son who deserved to have his father alive, sober, and present in his future. I had too much talent to let it become wasted in a cell or a cemetery. So, I followed the rules. I stayed in line, and I maintained my sobriety. I made it through my last detox, my last Clinical Stabilization Services, my last Transitional Support Services, and finally, my last residential program. I had a full-time job, I found a room, I got a second job, found a girl, got back visitation rights to regularly see my son, and soon enough, I was off probation. There was no more jail time hanging over my head. No more quick-fix, "spin-dry" trips to detox to start the whole process over again, no more visits to probation or random drug tests. It was over. I was done. This realization was both empowering and terrifying at the same time. Now that I had no one holding me accountable anymore and no threat of jail if I didn't stay clean, would I fall back into my own ways?

It lasted for a good while. I was working 16 hours a day and taking trips to New York, Florida, and Virginia about every other month. I wasn't taking the time to work on me, though. I hadn't continued to nourish the groundwork that I'd laid out to make it through in the first place. I stopped going to meetings and I wasn't saving like I'd planned. My prayers went from a comprehensive list of being grateful for every living person I could think of to a simple, quick, two-minute "Thank you, goodnight, Amen." Old habits, old behaviors, and soon enough, old consequences. My relationship was over. I quit one of my jobs then both of them. By mid-summer, I was using again. "How am I back here again?!" I thought.

I promised myself I'd never let this happen. With all the gratitude I learned in jail, all the blessings I received for working hard, all the memories of a nightmarish existence at 120 pounds, homeless, hungry, and slowly killing myself on a daily basis, I was right back to the same place I begged God to deliver me from four years prior. Was it all just a waste? Did I learn nothing from this tumultuous experience that I never wanted to relive again? No. Something in me clicked. Somewhere deep down, somehow, there was still a small semblance of a fighter that refused to quit and refused to give up. I didn't have any more of my nine lives left to use. I pushed it as far as it could go, and I knew the next time would be my last. I had to get out for good.

Guardian angels in the form of one of my closest friends from high school helped get me a job, and his mother offered me a temporary place to stay. I was working again. I had a safe, warm bed to sleep in, and I was clean. There's a saying in AA that has stuck with me for the last four years: "I know I have another relapse in me, but I don't have another recovery." This may be my last chance at life. I can't let it go due to one bad decision. I had to figure out what I was going to do with my future.

Aside from about a year and a half between Florida, Rhode Island, and Connecticut, I'd lived in Boston my entire life. It's safe to say that I had outgrown my hometown, and getting a fresh start somewhere new was imperative to maintaining my motivation. The decision to move away from the bitter cold New England winters wasn't difficult, but leaving my six-year-old baby boy was. I had finally been convinced to take his mother to court for visitation, and I actually won. I had been seeing him on nearly a weekly basis and was even able to have him overnight for the first time since he was born. This is what I'd been praying for, what I'd been wanting for the last four years, why I used to cry myself to sleep with a needle in my arm in my friend's living room and then in my jail cell at night for six months. How could I just pick up and leave him like that?

The terms of my living situation were coming to a close, and I hadn't even come close to saving up enough for the possibly $2,000 it would cost to pay first, last, and security for even a studio apartment anywhere around the Boston area. I was offered an opportunity to help pay the mortgage for a three-bedroom home on an acre of land that my girlfriend owned and live with her and her two boys in Virginia. It was a chance for us to start over again in a new place, away from Massachusetts, where we could develop new traditions, build a new community together, and begin a new, healthier future. I was going to miss my boy, but I'd figure out a way to visit as often as possible, somehow. Staying in Boston, where I would soon be homeless and jobless again, just wasn't an option.

A month later, I moved down South. I got a new job, had a new home, and was part of a new family. I think that's a pretty good start for someone who used to sleep outside or in random basements and steal food from CVS and Stop & Shop in order to eat. At this point in my life, the possibilities are endless. All I have to do is not use. This is my blessing. This is my plan. This is my Magic.

-Anthony Chaparro (late)

****The above piece was originally published in
"They Are Magic"
and submitted for inclusion by Blair Hayse*

Dear me (the many versions of me),

It's time, Nicole. It's time to let your voice soar. It's time to let your history resonate with the addict, the recovering addict, the child of an addict, and the addict's mother and father; it's time for the five-year-old version of myself to come to light. Fifteen and pregnant me, the criminal me, the prison me, the so-called recovering me, the wife, the stepmom, the daughter, the woman of God me. THE SOBER ME.

In this lifetime, we have had many roles together. At times, it's almost impossible to wrap my head around. Here we are 42 years old. To be 100% honest, the only reason we are still here is because of God and God alone. We're still here because God has a purpose for us. All the versions of us have battled to get to where we are today. The battles will never stop. That's okay because, with each new battle, we find a whole new part of us. A stronger us. We welcome to the battles today.

This life of ours started with addiction, darkness, and brokenness. Shall we share just a few of the life-altering moments with the world that sculpted us so long ago? Let's do it. My parents ran the streets of Miami, Florida, back in the 80s. My father and mother were a part of the outlaw motorcycle gang, and along with that were substantial drugs over state lines: organized crime, racketeering, and even murder. At four years old, I was taken and dropped off with my grandparents in North Carolina. I still remember so vividly that night. My father took me and said I would be staying with Granny and Poppy for a bit while he went and took care of some things. I can honestly say that I do not remember whatsoever when my mom actually left. She was hidden somewhere in the country. My grandparents and aunt raised me till the age of twelve. My family really could be considered the all-American southern family.

My grandparents provided everything a child could want or need. Tap, ballet, gymnastics, karate, and softball. I went to the same school my whole childhood and middle school. I didn't have to bounce around a lot. Though my family was there and providing everything, I still wasn't a happy child. As a child, my heart always hurt because all I ever wanted was what all my friends had, and that was my mom and dad. I was so envious of all my friends. My heart literally ached. I was so lonely as a child; it wasn't because my grandparents and aunt weren't there. I just always felt different and knew I was meant to be somewhere else. As I write this, I feel such conviction, and as you read on, you will understand why, if only I had known what my life would become later on in life, all because I wanted a mom. Children don't know any better, though.

When my daddy left me that night, I didn't realize it was going to be for eight years. When he left, he went and turned himself into prison. My dad never missed a weekend phone call. I looked forward to it every single weekend. For eight years, he would tell me the same childhood stories of him and his sister. And about me as a baby and anything else, I would ask him. He always reassured me that he was coming for me. It's crazy how so many things can happen in our lives and how a handful of them can scar your heart indefinitely. The first time I remember hearing from my mom, I was eight years old. I heard the phone ring, and my Granny answered it in the kitchen. A few minutes later, I heard my Granny calling my name. "Barbie, pick up the phone, it's your momma." All I remember hearing was, "You have a new little brother; his name is Bradley." Honestly, I don't remember if I was happy, excited, or envious and sad because he had my mom, and I was left behind.

Shortly after that call, my mom and brother showed up in North Carolina. I used to be so great with details. To the point I would be asked, " Do you never forget anything?" I assume the pain of the next year was so gripping I buried it as deep as the ocean floor. I remember Bradley spent the first year or so of his life at Granny and Poppy's house. I have the pictures as proof. I literally can remember everything, but this time in my life I just remember the announcement of my brother and when she left yet again. That year, I did know she was going to the community college and I remember she got up and made mayo sandwiches in the middle of the night. I can remember Rusty coming to visit Bradley and my mom. That's about it till she left. It wasn't till years later I realized her true intent of coming back there. One evening after dance class, my poppy picked me up. On our way home, he said, "Shug, we need to make a stop." We enter a tall old building; as we walk through the doors that evening, most of the lights are off, and then I see how neighbor who was a deputy at the sheriff's office. He says, "Bill, come this way." As we enter the room, I look to the right and see men in dark suits standing and blocking a doorway. The moment they see me, they step aside, and I look in the room, and there he is, my daddy. Oh my goodness, I do still remember 42 years later, that feeling of love and that big smile of his. He bent down and squatted, and I wrapped my arms around him and his smell. SAFE!!! At that moment, that little girl was exactly where she had wanted to be the last six years: in her daddy's arms.

He told me, "Baby daddy only has a few minutes." I didn't understand what was happening. He is leaving. No, I was so crushed. He reminded me of his promise. "I told you I would come for you, didn't I?" I nodded my head yes. He told me that it was going to be a little longer but that he was out and I would be seeing him more. My mom came back that year so she could help my grandparents battle this court case with my dad. She literally left right after. I do indeed remember that. I also remember her leaving and walking out the door. I tried following her and my little brother, but my aunt held on to me and said, "Barbie, it will be okay." It absolutely was not the fuck okay. How in God's name could she just leave me again?

Sadly, after some time, I still wanted to be with her. My family was hell-bent on me not going to my father's, though. I must have raised hell and changed after that because my Granny allowed me to go to Boise at the beginning of my fifth-grade year. That did not last long. My Granny got a call, and she was on a plane. She came and got me. That time, things didn't seem so bad for me. I do remember, though my mom and brother's dad were splitting up. So, what was the best way to get to my mom? That's right, calling my grandparents. And honestly they were valid in doing so. By my seventh grade year, though, my granny and poppy attempted the whole mom thing again. I will say this: I was so desperate for affection from my mom that I would endure anything. From the moment I arrived this time and walked into the house, I knew something wasn't right. I didn't care, though. I was done not having my parents.

I was a typical teen, so I thought. My mom was either gone a lot, or her boyfriend would say, "No, you're taking your kids." At the time, I thought it was cool. Hanging out with my mom's friends, having BBQs, and floating in the river. I even got a babysitting job with one of her friends, friends. It was actually her dealer's best friend. I was always babysitting and staying the night with her and her kids. Will just call her Danielle. When I wasn't with

Danielle and her kids, I was locked out in a living room with my brother, babysitting him and hanging out with whoever kids lived there. My mom started acting differently. Even worse than before, it just kept getting worse. She would be gone for days and return home, and then the fighting would start, and she would either walk out and leave again, or I was laying there hearing the fighting all hours of the night. It was one of those nights I overheard her boyfriend say, "Well do you have any more shit." My mom said, "Ya, it's in the stem of the piece." I had zero idea what she was talking about, so a few weeks later, I asked my mom's best friend's daughter what it all meant. She asked me if I really wanted to know. I said, "Yes." she informed me my mom was a dealer. Even then, I didn't understand what she was telling me. Then she broke it all down. I remember being so upset. But I was sworn to secrecy. Until I lashed out one night when she was saying I had to stay and watch my brother. I popped off and said, "What, so you can go do more meth?" She popped me so hard in the mouth, and I can say from that moment, there was no going back.

The life of betrayal, abuse, sadness, and darkness was upon me. We ended up moving out, and my mom got a little trailer and was living her life. I had started missing school because I couldn't take all the assholes and bullies. My thoughts were, well, she's not doing what a mother should, so why should I do what she says? Plus, the people who were coming over to the trailer all hours of the day and night were literally closer to my age, and that's because my mom's best friend's son lived with us. He was only four years older than me, he had social security, and he was obsessed with my mom. His mom was in a new relationship and she didn't want him messing up her new love life. So, it worked out for all people involved. Except me.

There were literally about seven of them who would come over all day, every day. They would ditch school and come to our house, and these kids were considered delinquents all because they went to Fort Boise. And they were all from Garden City. Garden City was then and technically even still now considered the ghetto. My mom decided to go to jackpot gambling for a few days with some new guy. She left me home, and Bradley was at his dad's house. Gene and all his friends showed up, and that night, a girl named Cayti showed up. She was a bit older, but maybe by eight years. She was different. She was what we would call normal. We became close and so my mom started to kick back some because Cayti seemed to be on the right track. That same night they came over one of Gene's old friends stopped by. I'll admit at fourteen, I was all giddy, and this guy showed me attention. We sat, talked, played video games, and played darts. That weekend was one of the best ones I had since living with my mom. Within a few weeks, I assumed my mom noticed me hanging out more in the living room and thought she would squash whatever was happening with us. At this point, nothing was happening. We ended up meeting up at our mutual friends' houses and we all just kicked it there. My mom tried her hardest to keep us apart. I hadn't even done anything whatsoever with him. Not sex or drugs.

We ended up becoming homeless again and living back at Gene's mom's house in a tent in the backyard. And with these circumstances, I spent most of those six months with Danielle and her kids. My mom found my journal in the tent and lost her mind; meanwhile, my mom, her best friend, and her whole family were packing to move to Alaska. I didn't think my mom was for real. She tells me I am going away to Jerome's for the weekend and to keep me away from him. She thinks sending me with two grown-ass men who are high was better. Seriously? We hadn't even left the alleyway yet, and Bill said, "You want some? I'm thinking, what is that? "It's a bullet," he says. He put it up to my nose, and he said, "Now snort," and that was my first time using meth. That whole weekend, I literally ate two bites of a slice of pizza. Aunt Kathy tells the boys, "You can't seriously take her back like this." I was out of my mind high. We pull up and my mom is just looking at me. She turns around, comes back a few minutes later, and wants to know what I want from Burger King. Mind you, she knew I was high, and she would always get so pissed I picked the most expensive thing on the menu, which I loved. This time, I was like, "No, I'm good." She brought the meal back and it sat in front of me the rest of the night. She slashed me with words that cut me deep and told me that we would be moving to Alaska within a week. Just like that, I left and stayed hidden till it was too late. The Alaska train was gone. She found me three days later at Danielle's. I mean, how badly did she really want to even go? She knew the only place I ever went was Danielle's house with her and the kids.

We ended up moving back in with my mom's longtime boyfriend, Dave was always considered my stepdad. And the only stepdad I have ever had. Now that my mom's best friend was gone, she was around more, and honestly, it wasn't better because I gave her hell in regard to the forbidden man. I wasn't out of control as a kid. I wasn't out smoking dope and partying. I was in love with a guy who had shown me attention. And we have to remember there weren't cellphones back then. So you waited and waited for the sound of a car to pull up or the sound of his base bumping as he came down my subdivision road. At some point, she gave in and allowed me to see him. And that was because if I was content, she could leave me home and go out on benders.

That summer, our friends Ron and Lindy got married. It was a morbidly hot August dry summer day, and they were having a freaking outdoor wedding. People were dying of heat. You would do anything to cool off. Schwan's almond toffee ice cream bar. Yuck! I hated toffee and I hated toffee even more once I puked it back up. I had a massive heat stroke. So I thought. A few days later, I was lying on my bed, and I looked up and over at my astrology calendar, the one my mom got me for my birthday from my favorite store called Eyes of the World. And it hit me like a ton of bricks that I hadn't yet marked my calendar for the day my period started. Every month for six months, I marked the first day and the last. And I'm on the 3rd week already.

I ask if I can go to his house. Which she absolutely hates because at this time in Boise, his house was known as the shack, and it was on Orchard. It's now condemned. But back then, you didn't want to be caught pulling out of that driveway. She said till eight pm then you better be home. When I got there, I told a girl named Misty what was going on. She took me to the clinic where you can get a free pregnancy test. It all happened so fast. The lady came back in and said, "Sweetheart, do you have any support or someone we can call for you?" I replied with, "No." That night, I didn't go home, and to my surprise, she didn't show up to get me. I remember telling him, "I'm pregnant." We were both in shock. And I wasn't ready to tell a soul.

Later that day, like a bat out of hell, she pulls in screaming, saying, "Get in the car, etc." I can tell she is coming down, and I absolutely do not want to go home. Once we get home, she will not stop ragging on me. I get it if I was an out-of-control kid. And considering I lived with drug addicts and I wasn't getting high, not even with him, I think I'm doing pretty well considering. And I can't remember what she said, but all I know is I snapped and said, "Oh well, guess what? I'm pregnant." I will never ever forget the next words that left her lips. " I knew I should've aborted you when I had the chance." That was it. I left and stayed gone. Throughout those nine months of the pregnancy, we lived back and forth between his mom's and mine. At one point during the pregnancy, my mom was interested in a guy, and he wanted her to move in with him. But how was she going to do that with him and me living in my stepdad's basement? Let me tell you how she did that. She convinced my stepdad to tell us that if he didn't move out, her parole officer was going to press statutory rape against him. And she knew if he left, I would follow suit. There's a means to an end with my mother.

Madison Gabrielle was born on March 30, 1998, and I couldn't believe she was mine. I was so exhausted from the labor and had to have an emergency c-section after fifteen hours of hard labor. I remember Danielle and her kids' dad came and brought flowers, and my mom left. That night, I just laid there holding Madison and thinking I would do anything in this world to protect her from the pain I had endured as a child. The first night I brought Madison home, I was terrified and basically alone. Everyone slept, and after about 2 hours of not being able to calm her down, my mom crept down the stairs and said, "Barbie, she can feel your stress." I didn't even respond because for me, I felt this was a moment a mother would help her daughter with helping her care for her new child. Let's not forget I'm barely sixteen years old. After a few nights, Madison and I had our little routine down. Madison was an easy child. And I supposedly needed to stop holding her so much, stop changing her diaper every time she barely wets her diaper, and lastly, "Barbie, if you keep bathing her so much, you're going to dry her poor skin out" and "Stop putting so much lotion on her." These comments are very important later on in my story.

By the time Madison was five months old, we lived with her grandma P between August and September while my mom was planning on moving back to North Carolina. She desperately wanted me to go. There was no way Madison and I were leaving her dad behind. The day my mom is leaving she stops by to say goodbye. She stays and talks for a few. She decided to ask if I would allow her to take Madison to North Carolina so Granny, Memaw, my mom, and Madison could get a generational picture. When I think about it, I still get so sick to my stomach and beat myself up mentally. That one day changed our lives forever. My mother proceeded to say, "Granny will fly her back within two weeks, and Barbie, I'll never do to you what Granny did to me." My Granny did nothing to my mom except raise her child while she was off living her life. Either way, why didn't I catch the signs then? Why did she even have to make that remark? Honestly, I never even thought anything bad. Why would I think our lives would be forever altered by this one decision?

It was time to meet my Granny the next day. When I stopped all these years later and thought about the communication with everyone while Madison had been back there for those two weeks, I didn't realize anything "off" about it till the damage had been done. I spoke with my mom the night before to get flight details. All she said was Granny, and Madison would be arriving around 3ish the next afternoon. 3ish became 4ish, and then became 5ish. We rushed back to the house to call and see if there had been an accident or anything. The phone rang and rang and rang. And if you know my Granny, that's out of the norm. After hours of calling, my mother answered, "Barbie, Madison isn't coming back and living in that mess." I was so blown the hell away and beyond confused. I was screaming, crying, demanding answers, anything. At that moment, my Granny picked up the other house phone and proceeded to say, "Barbie Madison will not be returning back to

Idaho." Still, to this day, I have to breathe through this because of the audacity, dysfunction, lies, deceit and hate that consumed me within. Like I said before, "There's a means to an end with my mother" She truly believed that her lies, this conjuring of bullshit would work. She didn't want to be out there alone, and the only way she thought she could get me out there was by lying about Madison's father and myself. When I say this is what created the beast, the monster, the deepest depths of darkness inside of me was this moment. My child literally being kidnapped from me. And to be honest with you, at sixteen, I had no idea what the hell to do, nor did her father. What I did know was that they had the same lawyer. The same lawyer who won against my father when he came back for me was the exact same lawyer now being used to keep my child from me. Do I feel in my heart now, after all these years, somewhere inside my family's hearts and minds, that they shouldn't have listened to my mother? Yes, how could they not?

The monster in me was alive and awake, and with each new day and more and more drugs, I was a lost soul. I had absolutely nothing to live for. Madison's dad was no help during this time. It almost felt like he wasn't affected by this, or he was just as lost as me, and it was like being a zombie and just existing. We could breathe and move but didn't know how to function or live. We loved Maddie so much; before this, he would go to work, and I would stay home with her. He would come home, and we would take her on walks and play with her out in the grass. She was our entire life. And now, just like that, she was gone. He met this guy at work, and he brought him home to hang out with all hours of the night. This guy had so much dope it was ridiculous. Then, of course, there was Danielle and her kids. When he was at work, I would be at her house. As I mentioned before, Danielle helped raise me, and I helped raise her kids, and now, with no baby and depression, all she and I did was get high all day, and then at night, we would all stay up getting high all night. I didn't ever want to go to sleep because it was in those moments of lying there attempting to sleep I imagined my baby lying in a room without me. It would literally devastate me to think about Maddie looking around for me or waiting for a hint of her momma's scent. And to know it was never going to be found for her was much to bear and or think about.

Everything I have told you so far doesn't compare to all the betrayals I have endured. I couldn't do enough drugs to mask the pain of everyday life. Before Madison was kidnapped. I was forced to have an abortion. Her father went back to his high school girlfriend while I was in Intermountain Hospital getting my medications stabilized. It was there I found out I was pregnant yet again. And my mom told me there was just no way I could stay with her if I was keeping this baby. I went alone. He left me at my lowest, and then he wondered why I did the things I did to him. From the age of 16 – 19, I ran hard. I had never stolen or anything like I was until I lost Madison. In those three years, I became an IV drug user and became pregnant again with my second child. Samantha Nicole was born on March 1, 2000. Before she entered this world. I had made up my mind I wasn't bringing her into this madness of addiction and brokenness. I had found a wonderful couple to adopt her. Her name was to be Rose. After Samantha was delivered, my mom and his mom pleaded with me to not put her up for adoption. They wanted to take care of her till I was able to. What killed me the most was I was doing the same thing my mom did. Having another child while my other one was without me. It made me physically ill to even think about it. The postpartum was real. As Samantha and I entered the house, darkness poured over us. I looked ahead of me, and there, taped to the top of the TV, was a loaded rig. With a sign that said, " Beam me to the moon, Scotty," that was my welcome home gift. I was repulsed. I took my baby to an unfurnished room and held her so tight, and she died inside crying. I whispered, " Please forgive me"

A few weeks later, I asked her father if he would watch her for 20 minutes so I could walk and get a pack of smokes. When I returned, I noticed some cars, and I bolted inside. The living room was empty. He wouldn't dare. I open the door, and there are people with needles hanging out of their bodies. I jumped over the bed and grabbed my baby. I walked outside and called her uncle, and I said, "Come get her; she can't be here." After she was picked up, I went to the bathroom. I got so high that my eyes started pouring tears. But not from me crying. It was my body reacting. I was going to make sure I wasn't capable of feeling anything.

I went wherever the dope was. I had never indeed been homeless before. I lost all sense of time or care in the world. One day, I went to drop some things off for Samantha, and her aunt asked if I would take her to see her dad. I took her to see him. When I walked in the door, I knew right then what had happened. Danielle and Samantha's dad had been intimate. I shouldn't care, but I absolutely did because she helped raise me. For God's sake, I would have to ask permission when I first started seeing him, for him to be able to come over and out when I was living with Danielle. I mean, seriously, how much more could I be betrayed and hurt by the people I loved? I took Samantha home, and for the next eight months, I was Ada County's most wanted. I refused to ever feel helpless again and on the streets with nowhere to lay my head. The girl's dad had taken the one person who I had turned to for all my teenage years. I met a crowd who were into white-collar crimes. We wrote checks, created checks, and created identities. For almost a year, Detective Lance Iverson searched for me. He raided so many establishments looking for me. I was getting exhausted, having to rip people off, create forgeries, whatever needed to be done so I could get a room for a night since I couldn't crash at people's places in fear that they would get raided because I had been there. One night, I was in my mom's basement, and we had spent over an hour waiting for me to find a vein so she could get high. The insanity. I put the needle down and said, "fuck this," and then slid to the floor and asked God when will all this end. I absolutely did not have the will to turn myself in. On October 7th, 2001, I woke up in the back of my friend's car, which never happened. I was always on point and ready to run. This time, I sat down and relaxed in the back while waiting for my dealer to get back to me to pick up. My two friends had answered my phone while I was sleeping and they went to meet him. So they thought was happening. Earlier that night, my dealer had gotten busted with some coke at the Motel 6. They told him that if he could get me to the Motel 6, they wouldn't charge him. The irony, though. A big-time dealer they let go just for me. I woke up in the back of the car, and when I came to, I looked towards the two front doors they were wide open, and no one was there, and then I noticed the blue and red lights behind the car. Lance walked up, opened the door, and asked, "So, who are you going to be tonight?" I replied with, " Me, just me."

I had three judges and 27 total charges. There were over 40 victims, I was told. Well at least the ones they were able to prove. I was sentenced to one year and eleven months with nine years' probation and court-ordered to the Christian discipleship home House of Ruth. Judge Neville, the devil is what he was referred to, told me that if I broke one rule at the home I would be sent back and do my full term. When you first arrive, there's a 30-day blackout period. Once that's done you can get a job and be put back slowly into the community. Six months was what I was ordered to so I am thinking I got this in the bag. On my first day out of the house, I reached out to my ex. Of course, he says, "Let's get a room." Honestly, this is not what I wanted, but I didn't say no either. We did end up having sex. As soon as we were done, I sat up and started crying. He looked at me as if I was crazy. I had such conviction because I knew I shouldn't be there, and I knew I shouldn't have had sex or even gone around him. Especially considering he was the first one who put a needle in my arm. The universe hated me. I was doomed from the get-go. Within a month, I was pregnant again. This time, I just could not do it. I was selfish and I called my dad and begged for his help. He wired the money to the clinic, and I took a bus twice to the clinic that day and terminated the pregnancy. I wasn't going back to prison. I was going to fight and get my kids back no matter what it took. My ex refused to give me a ride. He wanted the baby, and I hated him for that because he knew I would go back and do my time. That night, I just knew God was going to punish me. I was selfish and hurt another one of my children. I lay there and cried and cried. I didn't dare ask for forgiveness. My intentions were to look out for me and not go back to prison. That was the day after Christmas when this all happened. I just had to get to March.

Graduation day was here. I was done with the program, and now I can finally start my life and be a mom again. I started going to meetings every day. My parole officer wanted me to do 90/90. 90 meetings in 90 days. I said, "I'll do better than that." Somedays, I did up to four meetings a day. Shortly after graduating, I went to a meeting that I had never been to. As I was sitting there waiting for everyone to arrive so the meeting could start, I noticed a big crowd coming in together and one of them I noticed. We see each other. I stand up and give him a hug. He said it was so good to see I had finally gotten my life together. He said, " This is Russ,

Barry, and Mat." Mat was the loud "Hey, look at me type." His intentions weren't bad, though; he was just a genuinely outspoken individual. After the meeting, they all asked if I would like to grab coffee. I said, " Thank you, but no, I am good." After about a month of going to the meeting and declining all invites, I decided, hell, why not? Get out and live. Mat and I became pretty close we hung out a lot. But it was not like we were committed. But we did care about each other. And spent a lot of time together in the recovery community.

It had been about four months since I had met Mat. It was a Monday, my day off, and I had decided to go and meet a pretty special woman my roommate wanted me to meet. Kat Coe, we called her. I spent the entire day with this amazing Spiritual being and her brand-new twin babies. I had a tanning appointment that day with my best friend. I had forgotten my tanning lotion so we decided to swoop by my apartment. I ran up the stairs, and the house phone rang. I was just going to let the answering machine grab it until I heard Mat say, "Barbie, if you're home, I need you to answer, please." "Hello," I said. Mat told me he needed me to stay at the apartment and that he needed to talk to me. I was annoyed because he knew I was already late, and it was my only chance to tan that day. He insisted until finally, I was like, dude, just tell me, and as I was saying that, I heard a woman's voice that I knew. I said, "Why in the hell is my mom with you, dude." And a light bulb went off in my head. I demanded he tell me who was hurt, and then it just clicked, and I said, "Oh my God, tell me what happened to my daddy." Mat could only say, "I'm sorry, Barbie." I fell to my knees and curled up in the fetal position. The screams were so bad my best friend thought I was being murdered. All at once everyone must have gotten to my apartment at the same time because all I remember was being picked up and carried to my room and covered up on my bed. The shock within me was so surreal. Still, to this day, I can remember what the sky looked like at seven in the evening in Boise at the Vista Terrance Apartments. I can still remember the smell of that summer evening. As I have said before, there are those life-altering moments in life where you are forever changed and altered. Most assumed I would be running and gunning again because of my father's death. All I knew was that I needed to get right with God even more so I could see my daddy again someday in heaven.

After the funeral and all the arrangements and details and traveling were done, and I was back in Idaho, a reality had set in. That reality was that the only human that ever walked this earth who loved me endlessly was forever gone. The only human I could tell literally anything and everything to and who loved me no matter what was forever gone. I couldn't pull myself out of bed. The only time I did this was for my mandatory counseling. At one of the sessions, my mother was there, and she said, "Ya, I know God took the wrong parent." I didn't agree with her, but she has said that several times throughout these years. A bit of wisdom for whoever reads this. The night before my daddy was killed, my house phone rang. The phone was lying beside me, and I almost didn't answer because I was reading and it was late. Something nagged me to answer. "Baby, it's daddy. I just got up to use the bathroom and wanted to tell you daddy loves you." Please don't take the ones you love for granted. I am so guilty of this. My addiction also kept me from my daddy.

I truly believe God knows what he is doing. When God taketh, he also giveth. At the end of August, I was so sick and dehydrated for a week straight. I couldn't figure out what the heck was wrong with me. There was no way I was pregnant because God wasn't going to allow that to happen to me. Boy, was I wrong? I grabbed a test and took it. I couldn't believe what I was seeing. When I say Mat didn't believe it whatsoever, I truly mean he didn't believe it till almost six weeks later at my first appointment, and he saw the ultrasound. I believe with all my heart and being God placed that baby in my womb for many reasons. One to keep me pushing. I tried so hard every day to stay in the rooms of A.A., brush my teeth, and stay sober because I still had to get my girls back. I believe also that he was saying: "I forgive you." Those nine months were so hard, and I was still severely depressed; there wasn't a day I wasn't grieving or wondering how I could live in a world without my dad.

April 9, 2004. It was Good Friday. It was a planned c-section. I saw it as symbolic to have Alexis Eve on the day Christ gave his life for you and me. To top it off, my hospital room window faced Table Rock Mountain. The mountain that everyone all over Boise and Meridian can see from miles away, and on that mountain top was the cross that lit up at night. With all of this put together, my faith became stronger. Though my faith became stronger my and Mat's relationship did not get stronger. In fact, he had called off two wedding dates we had already set. One was while we were pregnant, and I had already bought my dress. He didn't marry me because his brother said, " If you marry her, I'll object." That is God's honest truth I have zero idea why he didn't want his brother to marry me. It seemed I was never good enough for his family or siblings. At the time, Mat was the black sheep child, you could say. Mat grew up LDS. For a while, I thought it was because of religion, but his brother was absolutely not active in the church. After that, Mat and I moved to Boise. Life seemed simple and normal, as normal as could be. I had Samantha back. We did struggle financially, but who doesn't. We had a close knit church family from the vineyard and were sober. Life was where it was supposed to be at least in the eyes of probation and recovery.

Mat's parents moved to Boise eventually and were close by for a few years. I had a great job at DIRECTV; he was working, and his parents helped with the girls. At this point, we had moved to Meridian and worked so much that we hadn't been to church in almost a year. Mat's best friend came into the picture, and his brothers lived three houses down. We were surrounded by alcohol. If you hang out at the Barber Shop long enough, you will get a haircut. I had to have dental work done and couldn't miss any more work. So, I had to take the pain pills, and I didn't want to because I didn't want to fall asleep. To my surprise, it was the complete opposite. Mat was drinking, and I started the pain pills. But I justified it by saying, "It's not meth"

We decide to move with his family to Nevada. The job opportunity was supposed to be better. The whole move was a mess. It took forever to find a rental, and in no way, shape, or form were we financially better. It was worse than ever. The drinking got out of control. The pain pills I wanted so I could clean and not feel so lonely. Mat would work four days on and then four days off. And when he was home, there was either a gathering of everyone drinking, or he was stuck in front of the computer and not really communicating. I had no friends, really. I joined the church and tried to belong but Mat and I were just living in two different worlds. I did communicate and say we need to do something. But I was talking to deaf ears. I eventually couldn't take it anymore and packed up the girls and moved back to Boise. I stayed with a friend and her family for a few months, and my girls and I stayed in her garage, which had been turned into a little bedroom. I got my old job back at DIRECTV and saved my money and finally got my own apartment. I was so proud of myself and living my best life. I had all three of my girls, and life couldn't get any better.

After a few months, I met someone. Things did move fast. I did what I had always done, though, and tried saving people. In hindsight I ignored the red flags on purpose and was just hopeful, I guess. I remember one day at work, I had run out of pain pills, and I wasn't tripping or anything. Why would I need to? Three days go by, and I am violently sick, and I don't know what is wrong with me. My partner says, "Dude, you haven't taken pills in days." I was like, so effing what. I said, "What does that mean." I had no idea people went through withdrawal from not taking pain pills. I assumed it would end quickly, but it wasn't, and sure enough, as soon as I got the pills, I was better than ever. I realized I couldn't go through that again, and one of my old acquaintances told me about the methadone clinic. I was so offended and said, " Bro, I am not a heroin addict." She said, "Are you serious? Opiates are heroin." Within a few days, I was at the clinic and working through the program, classes, and counseling…the whole nine yards. I didn't ever want to feel like that again.

I came home one day after work and realized the person I was with had moved out. No response, nothing. I was told that they were living with another girl named Madi. What a blow to my gut and heart. I couldn't believe this was happening. I thought all those red flags were just me tripping. Why was I not enough? What more could I have done? I closed the curtains. Crawled into bed and missed four days of work. I had enough doses from the clinic, and I was just going to shut the world out and keep myself and my kids away from all these people. I can't remember which daughter of mine called my mom and brother. One morning I woke up to my bedroom door swinging open, curtains being opened, and hearing, "Get your ass in the shower." I screamed at my brother to get the fuck out of my room, shut my door, and leave my apartment. He proceeded to ignore my request and then he said the next sentence that I will forever hate hearing." It's time to meet a real O.G., "I said, "What did you just say?" He repeated himself and said, "It's time to meet an original gangsta." I said, " I'm good and will pass on all that, thank you."

Later that evening, I received a call from my brother, and he stated he was two blocks away to come over and hang out. My kids were at their dad's house because it was summer. And there were only a few days left of summer. So, I forced myself to get ready and go. I wasn't in the mood, though, because I already knew that whoever he was chilling with was most likely using. And this is where the beginning of the end started for myself and my kids. I mean that last statement with every fiber of my being. I was introduced to everyone. They were all a few years younger than me but not much younger but I seemed so much more mature. And a lot had changed in "THE GAME" since I had last been running and gunning as it's called. It had been 15 years. And times just were not the same. The people, drugs, everything that comes with that lifestyle was nothing like it had been all those years ago.

I didn't stay too long. It was awkward and not my scene. A few hours later, my phone rang, and it was the person I had met earlier that day. I was asked if I could stop by their house and grab their bag and drop it off at the house where they were house-sitting. I said, "Sure." I always say I regret nothing because of this whole situation I regret more than anything. And the day I let Maddie go with my mom. I spent the next four years destroying anything and anyone who crossed my path. I ended up being in a relationship with that so-called original gangster. That person was not who I thought they were. Yes, I chose to relapse. I chose to decide to use. After the night I dropped that bag off and seeing what was inside, I didn't pursue the person. We chatted here and there over the next few weeks. Eventually, they showed up at my apartment asking if they could stay with me until their family could pick them up from Oregon. They said they were ready to get clean and sober and didn't want that life anymore. After being in Oregon for about two months and visiting once as a friend, I had a knock at my door one day, and there they stood. That's when our relationship started. And honestly things were pretty normal the first few months. That was until one day, after taking the garbage to the dumpster, they told someone where we lived. The person showed up at three AM, and then I was asked, "Do you care if I go and do some?" "Your choice," I said.

Eventually, after hanging out at the Barber Shop, I got a haircut. Obviously, so much more led up to this, but it's just too much to write and too painful. Someday, I'll get it all out there in detail. For now, I need to say that the fact I made it out alive is a miracle. I was so far gone and so deep in the darkness that I was absolutely sure I was not coming back from any of this, and I knew my children would or could never forgive me. I was ice cold in my heart. I had no heart. The only thing that mattered was bath salts. I loved that substance more than anything. I destroyed so many lives. I tortured people. I gave zero fucks about anything. I lost everything that ever mattered to me. And again, I was a means to an end for that person. And instead of fighting for me and my children, I fought to save someone that didn't deserve the same air I breathed. Never in my life did I think it was possible to be the way I was and all the things I did for that person and the drug. I will say this: in the end, I hated their existence and my existence with a passion.

Every bit of pain I had felt in my life I unleashed at the end of that last year. I was so alone and so beyond done that I didn't care if I lived or died. On January 28, 2015, I spent that entire day mentally tormenting a woman over a bag of dope. Back then it was the principle of it all. How stupid now. I knew I was going overboard but there was so much rage I couldn't stop myself. I had to be stopped. My karma came because when I had finally shut my toxic mouth, that girl got up, listened to where we were going, and made sure to call it in. When we were getting pulled over, I felt nothing. Literally zilch. I deserved everything I had coming at this point. I was sure I was going away for years because my life was out of control. Indictments, cartels, raids, you name it. When we got pulled over and asked for our info, I was sure I wasn't getting arrested. I didn't have warrants, and they weren't going to find what I had. A few minutes later, they opened the door, threw me down, put one foot on my back, and pointed a gun. I couldn't believe what was happening. Within minutes, the Feds were there, and they believed I was the getaway driver the previous December in a robbery at a store where two people killed a cashier. Yes, I knew who the people were, but anyone who knows me knows that I don't drive. It's my biggest fear. They had the wrong chick. The female cop shoved her hand down my layers of thermals, shirts, and hoodies. I was like, what are you mining for? Gold? Either way, they found the drugs, and that was that.

As the cell door slammed shut, I sat there like a zombie. I didn't cry; I didn't feel anything, so I thought. The moment the lights went out, it was as if the monsters within me opened the gates of hell and unleashed every single bit of pain and anguish I had been masking those past four years. I was ready to just be sent to prison and get on with it already. I didn't call anyone to let them know I was in jail. I received a letter from my mom that asked me to call her. So I did. She cried and cried and begged me to take drug court if it was offered. And I refused. I wasn't wasting my time or anyone else's and not giving false hope. It was too late, and if I was released, I would scour the ends of the earth for salt. So no, just send me away.

As I stood in the courtroom, my public defender informed me that they wanted me to take drug court. All I kept thinking was, why would they waste money and time? I am beyond repair. My kids weren't coming back, nor did I expect them to after the bullshit I put them through. The public defender also informed me if I didn't take the offer of drug court that, the judge would file the habitual offender against me. It's one thing to go to prison for five years, maybe. But up to 25? I was not willing or strong enough to endure that either. But drug court is nearly impossible. I had a week to ponder. As I sat on my bunk, my bunkie, who was actually a drug court participant and was there on a drug court sanction and most likely being discharged from drug court, gave me a bit of wisdom. And I have stood by this wisdom since that day. The best gift, chance, and opportunity I could ever give my kids was me being sober and of sound mind. I owed it to them to allow them the chance to speak their truth, no matter how ugly it may get. And it's true. Our kids owe us nothing. Also, even if they choose to never be in our lives again, we as addicts still owe it to them to be available so they may be able to heal. Not only that, she reminded me of who I was and still to be. I know I am an amazing human and woman. My heart is so full of love and understanding, and she reminded me that my mess is my message, and it's up to us as recovering addicts to allow our voices to soar and end the stigmas.

I entered into drug court on May 17, 2015, and yes, it was the hardest, most impossible thing to ever do. But I did it. I fell, I struggled, and I endured. Every day I would remind myself that I owe it to them to heal and ask questions if they so choose. There were so many days I felt the walls were caving in. But I had the desire to be sober. I didn't know what the hell my future held. And honestly, it didn't look too good. What support would I have, honestly? I had no contact orders with my mom and brother. Drug court was lonely. And I did break the rules and talk to my brother. When I spoke with him, he asked me to relay a message to his best friend. I told him it wasn't a good idea, and I reminded him that every time he has me reach out to one of his people, nothing but darkness comes from it. Of course, against my better judgment, I did it. I reached out to Scotty B. Anything I had ever heard of this man was to steer clear. Danger zone. As I type this, I can't help but giggle. At first, Scott was like why are you talking to me. Okay, jerk, never mind. Over the next few months, Scott and I got to know each other through Facebook Messenger. He got to know the real me, whoever I was, and still to come. We talked about everything. We finally met up. And the moment I first saw him, I was engulfed with butterflies. Yes, he was so handsome. But the way he looked at me. I still believe it's because he knew the deepest parts of me because, like I said, we would message for hours. And I was so reluctant to meet him. I wasn't willing to jeopardize everything I was trying to accomplish. I have a testimony of God's perfect timing. Scott and I had been in the same places for many years and didn't engage. In fact, I remember one day, my brother pulled up to my house with a guy. It was Scott. In the apartment I lived in when my daddy was killed, well, Scott was my downstairs neighbor. Crazy right? It's so true. God knew if we had met before now, we wouldn't be where we are today, and that's almost ten years strong and still going. Scott said he wanted what I had. He wanted to be sober and be present for his kids. He submitted to a random pee test with the drug court. We jumped through all the hoops that were asked of us. You are my north star, Scott.

I want the person reading this to know that recovery is possible. It's never too late. If you are alive and seeing this then that means God gave you another day. Keep going. All you need is the desire to be sober. Let the addicts hit their bottom. Stop giving them that parachute. Everyone's bottom is different. Everyone's recovery is different as well. Stop judging how we recover. Stop stigmatizing addiction, recovery, all of it. This country needs to open its eyes and realize it's not the addicts out there dying. It's our kids. A whole ass generation is being wiped out over fentanyl poisoning and accidental overdose; everyone should carry Narcan. It's a new household staple. It's dangerous out there, and we need to speak the hell up. Also, addiction is reaching almost everyone in this country in one way or another. So those addicts you are judging so harshly will be the recovering addicts showing your loved one the light to follow. To the parents still out there, it's not too late. Come home; your kids are waiting. Go home. Our kids are not better off without us.

To my Mom, I love YOU!!!! I forgive YOU!!!! I am so thankful you are still with us, Mom. I believe in you. You don't think you are a fighter, but I know you are. Mom, we have both made treacherous mistakes, but those mistakes don't define us. I know you have endured things that none of us know about. I want you to heal, Mom. Nothing is impossible.

Samantha Nicole, one of the greatest choices in my life was choosing to hold on to you, you have been one of my greatest supporters, and though this world has not been kind to you in your lifetime, that has never ever stopped you from loving endlessly, with every new milestone I pass, I always anticipate your love messages to me. You have evolved into this amazing woman who I am so beyond that I get to witness.

I am beyond blessed to have my children's forgiveness not everyone gets that opportunity.

To my husband and our six, out of this world, amazing kids, I LOVE YOU ALL!!!! I couldn't have done any of this without you all and God. Motherhood doesn't have an instruction manual, and neither does being a wife. But the past nine years have been the best nine years of my entire existence. Madison, Samantha, and Alexis, from the absolute bottom of my entire heart and soul, thank you for letting me be a part of your lives. Thank you for going through these healing and processing years. It has not been easy at all for us, but damn, it's all been worth it. Tre, Dru, and Mia, thank you from the absolute bottom of my heart and soul for accepting me and allowing me the honor to be one of your moms. You six kids will always have me by your side as long as God gives me another day.

Scott, I couldn't be prouder of you, my love. I know that everyone doubted us individually and as a whole. ten years ago, we had such darkness in our lives. But today, we are the light and it's up to us to shine bright for the addict who still suffers and for the newcomer. Keep going. Fall a million times and get up a million and one more times. I believe in you. End the stigma. Spread awareness and educate your loved ones. To another 24 clean and sober....

To the woman I was, I love you.

To the woman I am, I'm proud of you.

To the woman still to come, I'm so excited for you.

-Nicole Barker

I never thought of myself as the addictive personality type. I have never dealt with drug usage; I could pick up a cigarette to smoke when stressed and throw away the pack afterward…not picking another one up for months or years. Somehow, addiction was not on my radar, and I certainly felt I could not fall within its grasp. However, my life changed in early 2008. My husband, at the time, was charged with major felonies and later sentenced to up to 75 years in prison. I lost our home and every piece of furniture in it. I walked away with my two children and our clothes - and I barely got to take that.

I remember my depression spiraling out of control because I had recently had my daughter, and postpartum depression had been awful. However, due to his charges, I was under investigation by CPS for my children, and they had asked about me being on postpartum depression pills. Because I thought they were holding that against me and I might lose my children, I threw the pills away and quit them cold turkey. Nothing was going to stand in the way of my children. Depression slowly crept in full force. I had to force myself to go to work and to see my children. I had to force myself to eat or others did for me, because I would go days without eating. In just 30 days, I lost over 60 pounds due to stress and not eating. I began an unhealthy spree of survival mode.

Part of that survival was figuring out how to bury that grief and never think of it. So, I turned to my career. I was able to land a really successful job after I got my children's case settled. I began to throw myself into work. I would work non-stop. Of course, my boss loved it, and I was given bonuses, raises, and promotions. However, I was slowly losing grip on myself. I continued to lose weight until I was way underweight. My stress levels were high. I wouldn't eat much and lived off of coffee or alcohol. I could not sleep. The doctor gave me Ambien in its highest dosage, and I still could not sleep. I was having major migraines, so they put me on migraine meds. It wasn't long before I started to have seizures. Something I had never experienced in my life.

They ran tests for almost a year trying to figure out what was causing them, and it never was solved. I could not get them to settle down. They began to pile drugs on to treat it. I was taking nearly 12 to 13 pills a day to combat health issues. Stress was piling on with work and unresolved trauma. Did I address it? No, I felt like shoving it down and avoiding it was easier. I worked more hours. I took on more responsibilities. I would work day and night. Being on a salary, I could work as many hours as I wanted. No one was going to stop me from doing that.

Eventually, I had a mini-stroke. I will never forget that day because, by that time, I had grown accustomed to the seizures and had instructed those who worked for me not to call 911. They had threatened if I was taken to the hospital with one more seizure, they would revoke my license for six months, and I could not imagine that. So, I was getting used to the seizure activity. I continued not to sleep and to work all the time. Add to that all of the drugs they had me on, and I was a mess. One day, I was driving home from work, and I suddenly felt my right side go numb. I couldn't control the car. I ended up turning into the ditch of a friend's house. She immediately ran out and tried to help me exit the car, but I couldn't walk. She put me back in my car on the passenger side and jumped in. She told me she was driving me to the hospital. When she got there, they were trying to ask me for basic information like my name and date of birth. I knew what I wanted to say, but I could not form the words to say them. My mouth felt strange, and I could not talk. That was super scary. I was only 31, and I felt like I was dying. My friend gave them my information, and they immediately called for them to rush me back. Diagnosis: mini-stroke.

I am sure you think that would slow me down, but no, I worked more. I felt like I had to drown out health problems now. By the time I sat in a specialist's office to try to figure out why I was having these issues. He asked me how many hours a week I worked. I just said I didn't know - which was the truth. He was not accepting that, so he told me to go through my last week with him and tell him my hours each day. I sat there and did that. By the time I got to the end of one week, he said I had worked 120 hours. I had no idea it was that much. It didn't even feel possible, but there it was, staring at me from his paper. He then asked me how much sleep I was getting a night and I told him three hours most for several years. Usually between one to two hours. He put down his notes and looked at me... You wonder why you are sitting in front of me? If you do not stop working like this, you will not live to see 40. I was shaken because my kids already had lost one parent; they couldn't lose me.

So, I paused at work. Well, I tried to. I should get an A for effort. I moved to a lesser stress job in my field. I considered moving from the work career altogether but ultimately decided I could not. I spent the next decade trying to convince myself I was doing better and working less, but honestly, I still was a workaholic. I was addicted to it. I didn't feel accomplished unless I was working. I felt void. I felt like I was lazy. I had to face emotions and trauma. It wasn't until 2021 that I finally gave in. I am not sure if it was the traumatic birth of my youngest daughter, being diagnosed with fibromyalgia, or my cancer coming back, (probably a combination of them all), but I began not to answer my phone every time someone messaged or called. I silenced it. I would take baths without working through them. I began to put boundaries on my time. I started to sleep a full seven to eight hours. I began to take naps during the day if I was tired. It took several years, but I now lead a much more balanced life with work. I took toxic people and habits out of my life. I made room for things that filled me up and made me happy.

I have to remind myself daily. I have to deliberately tell myself I am going to be okay to take a break or a day off. I have to remind myself almost every moment that my phone can stay away from me - I now play games sometimes by letting my phone be in a different spot than me or going all night without even opening it. Addiction to work has been hard to break, and I turned it into an addiction to academics, which I had to stop as well. I literally dropped out of college because of how out of control the addiction was getting. Crazily, people do not understand how badly I was addicted, and they still get upset with me sometimes when I pace myself, but I am not taking care of myself. So, I will take it day by day, minute by minute, and continue to claim my life back. For me, it was a need to feel as if I had control in an area of my life when, in reality, I had zero control of that area now that I look back.

Addiction sucks, but I hope you will get help. Rehab was one of the best things I ever did for myself, and I am not ashamed to state that. Get help. Be accountable. And when you slip up or fail, don't spiral; acknowledge it and start back over again with the baby steps. Unlike other addictions, I can't quit working cold turkey, but I can learn to cope with my addiction daily and lead a better-balanced life.

-Blair Hayse

Additional Letters to Myself

(Trigger Warning: These letters portray someone who did eventually take their life, but are offered in a hope that one can see how others are impacted by losing someone they love)

Megan,

I watched as you came into this world; I swore at this world when you departed from it. In between, I held you through long nights of ear infections and fevers. I rocked you endless hours of sleepless nights. I watched as you grew into a young woman. I watched as the paths in life you chose stole your future for mere minutes of pleasure. I prayed to no avail that at some point, you would turn your life back to a path where life would bring you real happiness, not just moments of escape. You bore the weight of things that you couldn't control. You lived in a place of fantastic potential weighed down by the drugs that traded your reality for unachievable destinations.

I tried to make a difference in your life. I tried to be a father you could depend on. I tried to be a dad. I failed. I think back often to the decisions I made. I try to dream of how things might have turned in your favor had I done differently. I've come to see so much of you in the baby you left behind. There are so many conflicting emotions regarding the daughter you left for us to raise. You fed her your demons and left her for us to contend with. She didn't deserve the hell she suffered from her first months. And so I sat up rocking once again through the long night's hours of inconsolable torment. The sounds of hers and your cries ringing through my soul to this day. The future you gave up for minutes of escape, the future was stolen from this child to ever know your kindness.

Do I hate you for putting me in the place of trying to be a better father now, not getting to be a grandfather? Do I envy your escape from this tormented world of responsibility and betrayal? Do I surrender to that which is out of my control? Do I fight with you in my dreams or embrace the truth of your absence? The combination of emotions when I allow the silence to come is overwhelming. So, instead, I just keep providing the best I can for those who've chosen to depend on me for whatever reason. I squash the silence and cage the demons you've left me with. I wonder how much influence Mike had on you and your choice to follow him into the darkness of suicide. The two of you were so very important to me and you both chose to willingly tap out of this existence. I could succumb to anger, resentment, and sometimes envy. But no, that accomplishes nothing. So, in your absences, I continue trudging on with life. Looking for something I know will never be an explanation, a justification, consoling, a filler, the void of your absences. Some recognition that I have not completely failed you or Mike. But all I can do now is not become followers of you both, not put everyone through that torment again. Look for small glimmers of hope that Lillie will someday become a woman that you would be proud of. That's what I push through the days for now.

Just hoping that the scars on my soul left by you are overcome and that your child will never know your torment and my failure to save you from yourself. The conflicts are so many, so extreme, so torturous. They continue to go unresolved within my soul. The scars rip open as fresh wounds when I allow my thoughts to wander back in time. So much so that I don't revisit the darkness for fear that I will not be able to escape from it.

-Dad

Dear Megan,

I have tried to write this letter many times. I love and miss you beyond words. I never thought I could love a child that I didn't give birth to. However, you, in a moment changed that the minute I met you. You were accepting, loving, and the most kind-hearted person. I enjoyed getting to know you and loving you. I saw your heart and what a good person you were in so many ways, especially the time you devoted to loving animals at the shelter.

I often think of who you'd be today and or in 10 years. I am pissed at all the future things I won't get to share or see. I think of all the things you could have accomplished and never will on Earth. I read your journal, notes, and alphabet list on occasion. I get a glimpse of the pain and struggles you faced and were facing daily. With that, I want to apologize for all the humans that let you down and hurt you along the way. Most didn't do it on purpose. We talked about how hurt people hurt people, and that applied to you, too. I knew you didn't want to do most of the things you did, it was the drugs and illness. I forgave you, set boundaries, and loved you in spite of. You were loved and knew it. On occasions, it was not pretty but necessary for us both.

Your funeral was the first time many saw me cry. Tears for missing you, tears for not getting to see you mature, tears for not being able to see you free on Earth from the demons, drugs, and mental illness, tears for not seeing you have a relationship with Lillie, tears of lost the opportunity to be her mother, tears from the pain in your father and mother's eyes, tears from seeing how drugs and mental illness took you slowly over time that resulted in your choice to say no more and to end your life. I often think was the coward's way out or the boldest choice possible.

I thank you for the time we shared. The good, the bad, the ugly, and the gift of Lillie's life. You could have made a different choice, and you chose to have her. You had such dreams and goals for her and you. I can't imagine what it felt like to have your baby taken away without being able to see her for days. I am not sorry for protecting her from you, as we were doing what was best. I am so glad I got to see you hold her for the first time. Then my heart broke for you when we had to tell you that we obtained custody of her and she wouldn't be going home with you when you got out of jail. I hope you understand why we did what we did. I can't imagine not having my baby for a year and a half, knowing she was across town and not in my arms. The pain and suffering must have been horrible. I pray you understand the choice that was made. It was not a punishment to you, but a protection for Lillie, and desire it would motivate you to get it together.

Your father and I made a choice to take her, love her, and give what we could, with the hopes and prayers that you would get it together for yourself and Lillie to one day be the mother she needed. It isn't easy raising a child in your late 40s, you know. I gave up my life for Lillie and, in the process, lost mine, and my own child hated me. There were costs for your choices and ours. Some may last a lifetime. I fought and will continue to fight for Lillie to have the best life possible.

I changed the way I practice in my office, adding genetics to help others understand the side effects of knowing the best medications for their situation. I will continue advocating for testing and standing up for the underdog because of you. I will continue to see how shame costs you help at an early age and help parents remove the stigma of getting their children help no matter who knows. There is no shame in doing what's best. I am sorry you didn't get what you needed back then. Often, I thought, if only I had come into your life a year earlier, I could have made a difference. But grief does that, and hindsight is 20/20. I am not sure if I could have stopped you from the fate of choosing a permanent decision that day or not. Maybe if I had called later or come by. In the end, it would have just been another day if you really were going to.

The thought of you not being here when we are gone breaks my heart. The choice to end your life ended so many things for Lillie, too. We probably won't see her turn 50, her children graduate high school, and so many more things I can't even think about. She will live over half her life with no parent to guide her, support her, and help her when she needs it, and that breaks my heart. It is hard to get a lifetime of that in the years I have remaining, but I will do my best to instill all the wisdom I can. Allie has stepped up to the plate to be a surrogate mom to her now and when I am gone. She is kind, loving and simply the best person I know. She inspires me to be the best person and mom and will Lillie too. She will tell Lillie about you, me, your mom and dad, and how we all loved you so much. Your Mawmaw and Pawpaw were lifesavers when Lillie was little. They spent so many hours loving Lillie when your dad and I could not take another scream or cry all day and night. It was not easy raising a drug-addicted baby. It was years of hell, actually. It was one of the hardest things I lived through, but we made it. Lillie has been a Godsend to them as well. They stopped aging and are even healthier because of Lillie. They wanted to not miss a moment and haven't. When they don't see her for a week, they are calling. Just know Lillie is well-loved.

This July, Lillie will be 10. You would be so proud of her and all the things she accomplished. I often see you in her eyes, her movements, her love for music, her compassion for animals, her creative and artistic ways, her independence, her heart of love, and oh, how smart she is, just like you. I even see you when she doesn't understand why people throw trash on the side of the road, and she wants to stop and pick it up or give a homeless person money on the side of the road. I see you in so many ways in her. Thank you for her life and for allowing me to love you for five short years.

Someone once said to me there are far worse things than death. At first, I thought how rude and insensitive, but then I lived it. The sleepless nights, the wondering if you were calling from jail, the side of the road, and the police saying you were dead. There were far too many of those days, wondering if it was the day we'd get the call. When the call came in, there was sadness, disbelief, and also freedom from wondering when. We had a date, time, and moment when we knew we were all free from your addictions and illness. My friend was right, there were far worse things than death. Death was freedom for us, as it is for many others.

One day, I will have to tell Lillie about you and Jeff. It is not easy telling a child their mom and dad chose to live in a hotel. That your dad was twice your mom's age, and your dad fed your mom and you drugs and alcohol. It won't be easy telling her you chose to end your life while her father continued doing drugs and never once called to check on her and died from it. It won't be easy answering all the questions, and she will have many. We will have to relive all this all over again. I dread the question, why didn't she love me enough to live? I don't know how we will ever answer or if we will even have all the answers. I do know one thing: she will know she was loved and that you did the best you could. She will know all the ways she looks like you, acts like you, is smart like you, loves music like you, is creative like you, has that side look like you, and all the many good qualities the healthy version of you had. She will also know why and how you died, and she will be fiercely protected against repeating history. She will get help and has been in multiple therapies since birth. There will be no shame, only healing.

Until we meet again,

Tonya, your bonus mom

Messages Of Hope

We collected some messages from those who have struggled with addiction:

"What help/advice can you offer someone who is going through a similar situation?"

Here were their unedited answers to messages of hope they wanted to share with you:

Realize the addiction is not the final answer.

Addiction does not apply to just things that are socially considered negative. An addiction can be anything. Reading excessively is an addiction. You can have socially acceptable addictions, like shopping. Sometimes recognizing that what you are dealing with is an addiction, is the hardest part of dealing with it. When I was at the height of my soda drinking, I could drink two or three litters a day. It was just soda. It took me a long time to apply the word addiction to it.

If you have an addiction, don't measure it by what it is. Measure it by how much it is damaging your life. Then fight it any way you can.

Trust in Jesus!!

Self-awareness and honesty with yourself.

Learn how the conscious and subconscious mind work practice this material & build a life you are excited to live.

Seek help and find faith.

Seek help and keep moving.

For me personally not wanting for my children to feel the way I have my entire life. That's where I want to start with this question. I had already devastated them by my choices and my addiction. As much as I felt I only wanted to do this for them I knew deep down that it's never too late to start over. I knew there was a huge possibility they would never forgive me. I owed it to them to get my life together. So that in the future if they wanted to address me personally I needed to be in my right mind and ALIVE! For the addict who still suffers please know it will never be too late for you personally. Most of all the most important and crucial part of this journey is you must want it first. If you're not ready it's not going to work. And for the families who are affected by our inner monsters, there is absolutely nothing you can do to fix us. What our families can do is stop cushioning the bottom. The addict has to hit their bottom. And everyone's bottom looks different. Myself especially had to completely change everything about my life. Everyone's bottom looks differently, everyone's

Recovery looks different. The country and people need to stop stigmatizing addicts and recovering addicts. And most of all remember you have a purpose. And that with each and every storm that knocks you down you will get back up each and every time. Giving up is never an option. Feel the feelings, face the pain, trauma, uncomfortableness and heal.

Seek treatment and move forward with healthier lifestyle choices.

Appendix on Support Resources

Includes Links, Numbers, & Resources For Addiction

Find an AA meeting near you:

https://www.aa.org/find-aa

Debtors anonymous:

800-421-2383 – US Only

Underearners anonymous:

https://www.underearnersanonymous.org/

Narcotics Anonymous:

NA World Services

PO Box 9999

Van Nuys, California USA 91409

Telephone +1.818.773.9999

Fax +1.818.700.0700

Service Offices and Distribution Centers:

WSO-Chatsworth

1937 Nordhoff Place

Chatsworth, California

91311 USA

+1.818.773.9999

Fax: +1.818.700.0700

WSO-Iran

PO Box 14665-3115

Tehran, Iran

+0098.21886.81652

Fax: +0098.21886.7209

WSO-Europe

48 Rue de L'été

B-1050 Brussels, Belgium

+32.2.646.6012

Fax: +32.2.649.9239

Distribution Center—Mississauga

Ontario Canada

+1.905.507.0100 Fax: +1.905.507.0101

Al-Anon :

1-888-4AL-ANON (1-888-425-2666)

Gamblers anonymous

Phone: (909) 931-9056

Sexaholics Anonymous:

E-mail: saico@sa.org

Phone: +1 615-370-6062

Toll-free (USA & Canada): 866-424-8777

Overeaters Anonymous:

Telephone +1 505-891-2664

Workaholics Anonymous:

wso@workaholics-anonymous.org

Office: (512) 415-8468

Voicemail: (510) 273-9253

Caffeine Addicts Anonymous:

info@caffeineaddictsanonymous.com

Find support.

Appendix on Suicide Resources

Includes Resources for Suicide Help & Assessment

List of Suicide Help & Hotlines[1]:
(United States and Worldwide)

United States:
Emergency: 911
Suicide Hotline: 988

Algeria:
Emergency: 34342 and 43
Suicide Hotline: 0021 3983 2000 58

Angola:
Emergency: 113

Argentina:
Emergency: 911
Suicide Hotline: 135

Armenia:
Emergency: 911 and 112
Suicide Hotline: (2) 538194

---

[1] List of Helplines and Hotline Numbers Retrieved from blog.opencounseling.com

Australia:
Emergency: 000
Suicide Hotline: 131114

Austria:
Emergency: 112
Telefonseelsorge 24/7 142
Rat auf Draht 24/7 147 (Youth)

Bahamas:
Emergency: 911
Suicide Hotline: (2) 322-2763

Bahrain:
Emergency: 999

Bangladesh:
Emergency: 999

Barbados:
Emergency: 911
Suicide Hotline Samaritan Barbados: (246) 4299999

Belgium:
Emergency: 112
Suicide Hotline Stichting Zelfmoordlijn: 1813

Bolivia:
Emergency: 911
Suicide Hotline: 3911270

Bosnia & Herzegovina:
Suicide Hotline: 080 05 03 05

Botswana:
Emergency: 911
Suicide Hotline: +2673911270

Brazil:
Emergency: 188

Bulgaria:
Emergency: 112
Suicide Hotline: 0035 9249 17 223

Burundi:
Emergency: 117

Burkina Faso:
Emergency: 17

Canada:
Emergency: 911
Suicide Hotline: 1 (822) 456 4566

Chad:
Emergency: 2251-1237

China:
Emergency: 110
Suicide Hotline: 800-810-1117

Columbia:
24/7 Helpline in Barranquilla: 1(00 57 5) 372 27 27
24/7 Hotline Bogota: (57-1 323 24 25

Congo:
Emergency: 117

Costa Rica:
Emergency: 911
Suicide Hotline: 506-253-5439

Croatia:
Emergency: 112

Cyprus:
Emergency: 112
Suicide Hotline: 8000 7773

Czech Republic:
Emergency: 112

Denmark:
Emergency: 112
Suicide Hotline: 4570201201

Dominican Republic:
Emergency: 911
Suicide Hotline: (809) 562-3500

Ecuador:
Emergency: 911

Egypt:
Emergency: 122
Suicide Hotline: 131114

El Salvador:
Emergency: 911
Suicide Hotline: 126

Equatorial Guinea:
Emergency: 114

Estonia:
Emergency:112
Suicide Hotline: 3726558088
In Russian: 3726555688

Ethiopia:
Emergency: 911

Finland:
Emergency: 112
Suicide Hotline: 010 195 202

France:
Emergency: 112
Suicide Hotline: 0145394000

Germany:
Emergency: 112
Suicide Hotline: 0800 111 0 111

Ghana:
Emergency: 999
Suicide Hotline: 2332 444 71279

Greece:
Emergency: 1018

Guatemala:
Emergency: 110
Suicide Hotline: 5392-5953

Guinea:
Emergency: 117

Guinea Bissau:
Emergency: 117

Guyana:
Emergency: 999
Suicide Hotline: 223-0001

Holland:
Suicide Hotline: 09000767

Hong Kong:
Emergency: 999
Suicide Hotline: 852 2382 0000

Hungary:
Emergency: 112
Suicide Hotline: 116123

India:
Emergency: 112
Suicide Hotline: 8888817666

Indonesia:
Emergency: 112
Suicide Hotline: 1-800-273-8255

Iran:
Emergency: 110
Suicide Hotline: 1480

Ireland:
Emergency: 116123
Suicide Hotline: +4408457909090

Israel:
Emergency: 100
Suicide Hotline: 1201

Italy:
Emergency: 112
Suicide Hotline: 800860022

Jamaica:
Suicide Hotline: 1-888-429-KARE (5273)

Japan:
Emergency: 110
Suicide Hotline: 810352869090

Jordan:
Emergency: 911
Suicide Hotline: 110

Kenya:
Emergency: 999
Suicide Hotline: 722178177

Kuwait:
Emergency: 112
Suicide Hotline: 94069304

Latvia:
Emergency: 113
Suicide Hotline: 371 67222922

Lebanon:
Suicide Hotline: 1564

Liberia:
Emergency: 911
Suicide Hotline: 6534308

Luxembourg:
Emergency: 112
Suicide Hotline: 352 45 45 45

Madagascar:
Emergency: 117

Malaysia:
Emergency: 999
Suicide Hotline: (06) 2842500

Mali:
Emergency: 8000-1115

Malta:
Suicide Hotline: 179

Mauritius:
Emergency: 112
Suicide Hotline: +230 800 93 93

Mexico:
Emergency: 911
Suicide Hotline: 5255102550

Netherlands:
Emergency: 112
Suicide Hotline: 900 0113

New Zealand:
Emergency: 111
Suicide Hotline: 1737

Niger:
Emergency: 112

Nigeria:
Suicide Hotline: 234 8092106493

Norway:
Emergency: 112
Suicide Hotline: +4781533300

Pakistan:
Emergency: 115

Peru:
Emergency: 911
Suicide Hotline: 381-3695

Philippines:
Emergency: 911
Suicide Hotline: 028969191

Poland:
Emergency: 112
Suicide Hotline: 5270000

Portugal:
Emergency: 112
Suicide Hotline: 21 854 07 40
And 8 96 898 21 50

Qatar:
Emergency: 999

Romania:
Emergency: 112
Suicide Hotline: 0800 801200

Russia:
Emergency: 112
Suicide Hotline: 0078202577577

Saint Vincent and the Grenadines:
Suicide Hotline: 9784 456 1044

São Tomé and Príncipe:
Suicide Hotline: (239) 222-12-22 ext. 123

Saudi Arabia:
Emergency: 112

Serbia:
Suicide Hotline: (+381) 21-6623-393

Senegal:
Emergency: 17

Singapore:
Emergency: 999
Suicide Hotline: 1 800 2214444

Spain:
Emergency: 112
Suicide Hotline: 914590050

South Africa:
Emergency: 10111
Suicide Hotline: 0514445691

South Korea:
Emergency: 112
Suicide Hotline: (02) 7158600

Sri Lanka:
Suicide Hotline: 011 057 2222662

Sudan:
Suicide Hotline: (249) 11-555-253

Sweden:
Emergency: 112
Suicide Hotline: 46317112400

Switzerland:
Emergency: 112
Suicide Hotline: 143

Tanzania:
Emergency: 112

Thailand:
Suicide Hotline: (02) 713-6793

Tonga:
Suicide Hotline: 23000

Trinidad and Tobago:
Suicide Hotline: (868) 645 2800

Tunisia:
Emergency: 197

Turkey:
Emergency: 112

Uganda:
Emergency: 112
Suicide Hotline: 0800 21 21 21

United Arab Emirates:
Suicide Hotline: 800 46342

United Kingdom:
Emergency: 112
Suicide Hotline: 0800 689 5652

United States:
Emergency: 911
Suicide Hotline: 988

Zambia:
Emergency: 999
Suicide Hotline: +260960264040

Zimbabwe:
Emergency: 999
Suicide Hotline: 080 12 333 333

Conduct a Suicide Inquiry[2]

a. **Ideation**

Frequency, Intensity and Duration

- Have you had thoughts of hurting yourself or others?
- Have you thought about ending your life?

Now, in the Past, and at its Worst

- During the last 48 hours, past month, and worst ever: How much? How intense? Lasting for how long?

b. **Plan**

Timing, Location, Lethality, Availability/Means

- When you think about killing yourself or ending your life, what do you imagine?
- When? Where? How would you do it? In what way?

---

[2] Retrieved from Minnesota Department of Health at: https://www.health.state.mn.us/people/syringe/suicide.pdf

Preparatory Acts

- What steps have you taken to prepare to kill yourself, if any?

c. Behavior

Past attempts, aborted attempts, rehearsals

- Have you ever thought about or tried to kill yourself in the past?
- Have you ever taken any actions to rehearse or practice ending your life (e.g., tying noose, loading gun, measuring substance)?

Non-suicidal self-injurious behavior

- Are you having paranoid thoughts? Hallucinations?
- Have you done anything to hurt yourself (e.g., cutting, burning or mutilation)?

d. Intent

Extent to which they expect to carry out the plan and believe the plan to be lethal versus harmful.

- What do you think will happen?
- What things put you at risk of ending your life or

killing yourself (reasons to die)?
- What things prevent you from killing yourself and keep you safe (reasons to live)?

Explore ambivalence between reasons to die and reasons to live. Pay attention to how they describe the outcome.
- "I'm dead, it's over." indicates a higher risk of suicide death.
- "I think I'd end up in the hospital." indicates a moderate risk of suicide death.
- "I don't want to die; I want my suffering to end." indicates a lower risk of suicide death.

e. **Notes**

- When working with **youth**, collect information from a parent, guardian or service provider on the youth's suicidal thoughts, plans, behaviors, and changes in mood, behavior or disposition.
- If the person has thoughts or plans to **harm someone else**, conduct a homicide inquiry using the same questions (replace "hurt or kill yourself" with "hurt or kill someone else").

Determine Risk Level[3]

The risk level is determined with the previous three steps:

1. Risk Factors
2. Protective Factors
3. Suicide Inquiry

Death by Suicide Risk Level

Risk Level	Risk Factors	Protective Factors	Suicide Inquiry	Intervention*
High	Multiple risk factors	Protective factors are not present or not relevant at this time	Potentially lethal suicide attempt or persistent ideation with strong intent or suicide rehearsal	Hospital admission generally indicated, suicide precautions (e.g., observation, means reduction)
Moderate	Multiple risk factors	Few protective factors	Suicidal ideation with a plan, but not intent or behavior	Hospital admission may be necessary, develop crisis plan and suicide precautions, give emergency/crisis numbers

---

[3] Retrieved from Minnesota Department of Health at: https://www.health.state.mn.us/people/syringe/suicide.pdf

Low	Few and/or modifiable risk factors	Strong protective factors	Thoughts of death with no plan, intent or behavior	Outpatient referral, symptom reduction, give emergency/crisis numbers

Take every suicide attempt seriously!

People often think a person is not really suicidal.

It's better to be safe, even if they will be angry with you for taking action to keep them alive.

About the Author

Jen Taylor, LCSW
#1 International Bestselling Author

Jen Taylor, LCSW is a New York-based spiritual psychotherapist with 23+ years of experience. Jen specializes in womens' empowerment, domestic violence, teens, and LGBTQIA+ individuals. Jen incorporates spirituality and astrology into her sessions to create a truly unique blend of guidance.

Jen was born and raised in New York City and lived there from preschool through high school. Instead of attending her prom, Jen went to boot camp for the Navy and received accreditation as a U.S. Naval photographer. Jen then received her Bachelor's in Arts from Haverford College in Pennsylvania and studied abroad in Florence, Italy. She spent her early 20s in the advertising office of Italian *Vogue* and went on to attend social work school at Fordham University's Graduate school of social services. In 1999, Jen received her Master's in social work while pregnant with her first child, Giancarlo. Jen worked in various outpatient mental health clinics in New York City, and in 2007 had her second child, Elisabetta.

Jen Taylor, LCSW is the editor for Girl on Fire Magazine's "Wine Down with Jen," where she uses her 20+ years of experience as a New York-based spiritual psychotherapist to bring you cozy couch conversations you would have with your best friend over a glass of wine after work.

When not writing for the magazine or seeing clients, Jen enjoys traveling, photography, spending time with her kids, and a good cup of coffee.

Jen is a multiple #1 International bestselling author in a collaboration series and currently working on releasing the rest of this series as her very first solo books over the next year.

To connect with Jen, she can be reached at:

Jentaylorfani@gmail.com

www.ingramcontent.com/pod-product-compliance
Lightning Source LLC
LaVergne TN
LVHW051953060526
838201LV00059B/3617